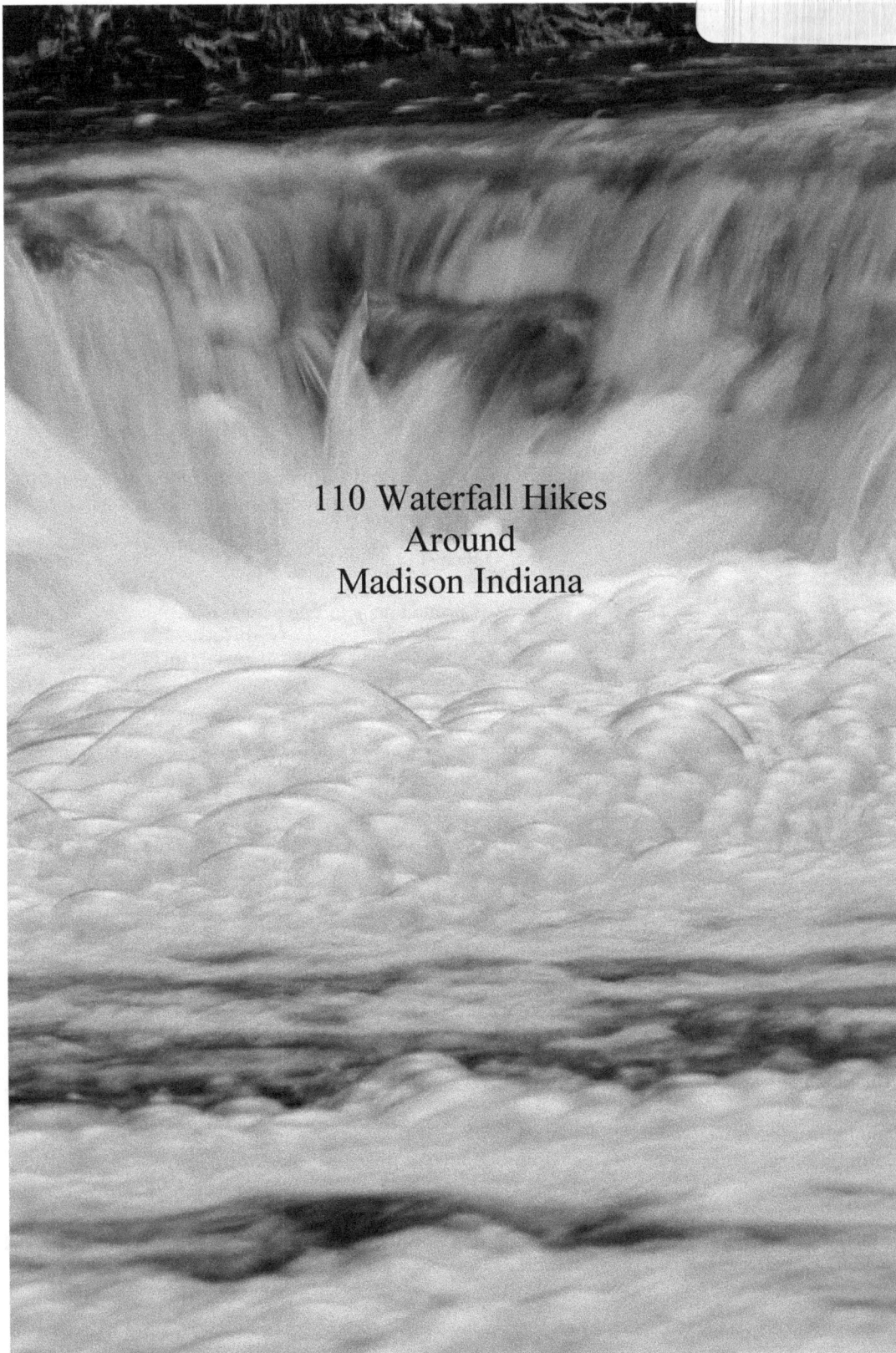

110 Waterfall Hikes
Around
Madison Indiana

Tina Karle

ISBN: 978-1-257-80519-8

This book is printed on acid free paper.

Printed in the United States of America

Lulu Publishing
North Carolina
www.lulu.com

Front Cover Waterfalls: Brushy Creek, White Road Falls, Schoolhouse Falls, Butler Falls, Camp Creek Falls, Zion Cemetery Falls, Hanging Rock, Thornton Road Falls, Deadmans Falls, and Crooked Creek Main Falls

Acknowledgements

I would like to give thanks to GOD for giving us these beautiful falls to enjoy. Also special thanks to my husband for all his patience in the many hours of driving the country roads to find these falls for all to enjoy!

Disclaimer

This book is written to the best of the author's knowledge of known waterfalls. Some waterfalls are on private property. You must obtain permission before seeing such falls. The author disclaims any liability from any accidents occurring while using this book as a guide. Most all trails listed in this book are safe to traverse. Take heed of certain trail conditions as they can change drastically from unknown weather conditions and you are cautioned to not place undue acceptance of all knowledge in this book and to use this guide at your own risk!

Tina Karle

Table of Contents

Excerpt from the Author 7
Foreword 9
Introduction 11
Hiking Key Page 19
Rating System 21
Before You Begin You're Hike 22

Madison Hikes 23
Aberdeen Road Falls 24
Alcove Falls 25
Arnold Creek Falls 26
Brown Road Falls 27
Brushy Creek Falls 28
Bull Creek Falls 29
Butler Falls 30
Cali Nature Preserve 32
Camp Creek Falls 34
Camp Meeting Road Falls 35
Chain Mill Falls 36
Clifty Falls 37
Crooked Creek Falls 45
Crosley Lake Falls 46
Deadmans Falls 48
Deer Path Falls 50
Dry Falls 51
Dry Fork Creek 52
Dugan Hollow Road Falls 53
Eagle Hollow Falls 54
Farmers Retreat Falls 55
Hanging Rock Falls 57
Hanover Beach Hill Falls 58
Hatcher Hill Falls 60
Huckleberry Branch Falls 62
Indian Kentuck Cemetery 63
Little Bull Creek Falls 65
London Road Falls 67
Lost Fork Road Falls 68
Lowry Lane Falls 69
Lucina Ball Drive Falls 70
Michigan Road Falls 71
Muscatatuk County Falls 72
Old State Route 62 74
Olean Cemetery Falls 75
One Lane Road Falls 76
Route 3 Falls 77
Route 7 Falls 78

110 Waterfall Hikes Around Madison Indiana

Route 56 Falls — 80
Route 62 Falls — 81
Route 421 Falls — 82
Scenic Drive Falls — 83
Signor Hill Road Falls — 84
Sunrise Golf Course — 85
Sweet Water Road Falls — 88
Thorton Road Falls — 89
Tull Road Falls — 91
Vulture Falls — 92
White Road Falls — 93

GPS Only Hikes — 94
Barking Dog Falls — 95
Bascom Corner Falls — 96
Bear Valley Road Falls — 97
County Road 125 S — 98
County Road 325 Falls — 99
County Road 950 Falls — 100
Cragmont Street Falls — 101
Crooked Creek Main Falls — 103
Crowe Falls — 104
Dobson Hollow Falls — 106
Dugan Hollow Falls — 107
E 1033 Road Falls — 108
Fremont Falls — 109
Harts Falls — 110
Hebron Cemetery Falls — 112
Hidden Falls — 114
Horseshoe Falls — 116
K Road Falls — 117
Long Branch Falls — 119
McIntyre Road Falls — 120
New Prospect Cemetery — 122
Overhang Falls — 124
Overturf Cemetery Falls — 125
Pumphouse Falls — 126
Quercus Grove Falls — 127
Route 129 Falls — 128
Schoolhouse Falls — 129
Zion Cemetery Falls — 131

Mini Waterfalls — 132
300S Road Falls — 133
650 S Road Falls — 134
Barkworks Road Falls — 135
Bear Branch Falls — 136
Bear Creek Falls — 137
Bee Camp Creek — 138
Boyd Branch Falls — 139

Tina Karle

County Road 275 Falls	140
County Road 650 S Falls	141
County Road 40 Falls	142
Dry Fork Road Falls	143
Hard Scrabble Road Falls	144
Horton Hollow Falls	145
Iceberg Road Falls	146
Indian Creek Falls	147
Indian Kentuck Creek Falls	148
Little Brushy Fork	149
Little Creek Falls	150
Long Run Falls	151
Mennets Hollow	152
Pendelton Run Falls	153
Peter Creek	154
Raccoon Creek Falls	155
Route 262 Falls	156
Salem Branch Falls	157
South Fork Falls	158
Tate Ridge Road Falls	159
Toddy's Creek Falls	160
Turkey Run	161
Uhlman Creek Falls	162
Waterloo Road Falls	163
West Fork Falls	164
Wolf Run	165
Bibliography	166
Waterfalls By Area	167
Index	170
About the Author	172

Excerpt from the Author

Do you know my friend? I would like to introduce you to someone who is dear to me! But first, I know right? A hiking book, an odd place to put something like this. But this is a subject that I felt was important to share with you the reader. I want you to meet my friend Jesus. Now before the eye rolling starts and the stutters and curses start to flow, I'd like you to hear me out. For not many seem to know my Jesus. Yes it is the same one that was born in a lowly manger to a virgin daughter of Abraham. Mary was her name. By her obedience to Father God in accepting a huge challenge, her simple acquiescence to be the hand maid of the Lord rocked this world. It brought forth our savior. What? Don't believe that a child was born without a father to do the act? Ah but that is where miracles begin my friend. For Jesus' birth was a miracle. His birth caused a king to slaughter thousands of innocent infants from a devils rage to stop God's plan from happening. But God was with him. He survived and grew. Was tempted like we are and yet was without sin. They tortured and hung him on a cross; a common criminal if you please. But, on that wondrous third day he rose again in fulfillment of what He said would come to pass. It was written that that would happen in several places in the bible. Ah yes that book, that one that has been sitting on a shelf somewhere. Little used and dusty. It's in there though. That book, it is Jesus' for He is the Word; part of the Trinity. He came to earth to be a man. To become human to share in our pain and daily sufferings. He became man to understand us better, to know and understand our feelings and what we go through. Think he's just a myth, a fairy tale? Not important anymore? Well here is where I beg to differ. I know some of you will not share my views and will probably slander what I am saying here but I must share my thoughts. Read on if you are still curious to know the person whom I cannot live without. For you see, Jesus is the friend I've always wanted. He longs to have a relationship with everyone, not just me. I met him one day you see quite by accident and it changed my life. He can and will change yours if you let Him. I really wasn't looking for Him but He was looking for me. He got my attention in very subtle ways. Oh I thought I knew Him, having been brought up catholic. I read the children's stories, heard the Easter story and seen the movies. But that was face value stuff. That doesn't really show you who Jesus really is. Some may think so but I'm here to tell you its not. Having known about Jesus all my life I thought I knew about him but I came to find out one evening, I didn't know him at all. For you see I was content in my life in how I was living and all I was doing at the time. But that was when God got my attention. He had a plan for me you see, just as He does for each of you. It was time I guess I woke up to the plan He had for me in my life. So He slowly and subtly got my attention in little ways. An accident to me at work, meant to harm me came out to be used for God's good plan. In my convalescence doing light duty work God came and got my attention. It had happened before you see and I paid it a small mind but that night walking down that hallway to the ladies room, God woke me up to who He is. For He gave me a jolt you see something hard to explain with mere words. But from that moment on my life changed. From that moment life sped up for me, even though it was still the same day to day grunge, events started happening. A job change, my marriage put back to rights, relationships with friends changed, and time when I didn't have hardly a friend left I met Jesus. Working at the IRS came the opportunity to listen to music and books on tapes. I stumbled across a person who knows my Jesus. I listened to his funny stories about life and how he was slowly introducing me to a Jesus I didn't know. But, I wanted to know better! Jesse Duplantis changed my thoughts on what I thought I knew about Jesus. So deciding to go back to church with my husband, I committed myself one evening to surrendering to accept Jesus into my life. From that moment on my life changed. Staying in church and learning who I really was helped to mold me into who I am today. Oh I'm guilty of leaving my home church for two years and going to a lesser church. But in those two years God used me and molded me and made me hunger for more of what I didn't understand. Going back to my church where I was saved helped turn me in the right direction. For you see it is all a choice. I myself can't make you accept Jesus. That is for you to decide yourself. I am just a messenger come to share what He's done for me. Although in church you receive do's and dont's about how to live and what you should and shouldn't do once you are a Christian. These are important for boosting your faith. To some that is a drag. But it will help mold you to what Jesus says in His Word. My Jesus you can learn about that way to an extent which is good too, but it's the personal relationship I'm wanting to impart to you. That is something not often taught in church. For God wants to know us on a personal level. How you are wondering? Let me share with you how

Tina Karle

to know God and Jesus in a way He wants to be known. Hence why I am writing all this so called boring stuff to you. Did you realize it is a simple matter? People make it hard all the time when actually the matter is very simple, for it is simple you see! Most have put Jesus in a box. Not knowing that's what they've done. They take Him out on Sunday and put Him back again that night to maybe think about Him some during the week. Harsh? Maybe, but with many that is truth. They don't want Him interfering in "their" life. Not knowing that Jesus is a gentleman, He won't interfere. He will stand aside and let them do their own thing. Till they mess up and then want to pull him out of that box with their cry for help. He wants to share with you your every day things, did you know that? He wants you to talk with him about your problems, your relationship issues that are stagnant, your loneliness in not having a friend, or in your marriage issues. He wants to share in your triumphs and hold you when you're sad. He's there to pick you up when you're down and have you lean on Him when you can't fight no more. That's when He wants you to give it all to Him so He can fight for you. He's all around His very presence in the smallest things. Hard to believe but that's the power He has. From being creator of this our world yet humble and powerful enough to live inside of us. That itself is a mystery one in which I myself can't explain but simply accept. Ah but I digress. This book is meant to show you Jesus and God in a different way if you will allow Him too. For in this book you will see His handiwork everywhere. He made all of those wonderful things for us to enjoy. I have put it into book form for you to get a glimpse of the power and majesty He brought for us to enjoy. For I believe waterfalls and the knowledge about them is a calling He has given to me to share with you the reader to enjoy. In creating this book while walking the woods, He was there beside me every step of the way; guiding me to the next set of falls. How did I find these falls you ask? I give all the glory to God and Jesus. For all I simply did was use topography maps and ask Jesus to come with me for the day. To guide me to the falls He wanted people to see. Whatever is hidden will be made known to those who wish to see. His gentle guidance in things not often seen right in front of us is why this book came to be. Same with all my other books. Things we take for granted and no longer see. Same with Jesus. Taken for granted, not really seen for who He really is. Let this book be a guide to show you a little bit of Him. Ask Him to go for a walk with you in the woods that are listed here in this book. Talk to Him while on that walk. Like you would a good friend. Don't think yourself crazy talking out loud to no one for He will be there walking beside you rejoicing that you chose to acknowledge Him. You may not physically with your ear hear His comment to you, but He will reveal Himself in many ways. A lovely bird song, a deer stepping out of the woods near you, a lone beautiful flower all speak of His nearness to you. The rustle of the wind in the trees or the scent laden breeze tickling your face, all speak of His presence to woo you to Him. Will you let him woo you? As He did me? He's right there, always a gentleman, waiting to take your hand and walk that sunny path called life. It may contain clouds and some dreary days and may perhaps lead down into a dark hollow but hold tight to His hand and He'll lead you back to that sunny bright path leading to that waterfall tripping and skipping along. A voice you may hear in the chattering of the water may just be what you need to hear. So let this book be that guide to hear His voice in a way you've not heard before....

If you would like to invite Jesus into your heart to be with you always simply say these words to start on a new path for a better and richer life.....
As you say these words, if you'll believe them with your heart, you will be born again (Romans 10:9-10)
Jesus, come into my life. Forgive me of all my sins. I ask you to cleanse my heart, and make me a new person in You right now. I believe that You are the Son of God and that You died on the cross for me. Jesus, I want to thank you for loving me enough to die for me. I accept all that Your shed blood bought for me on the cross, and I receive You as my Savior and Lord. In Your name I pray. Amen.
If you just prayed this prayer, congratulations! You are a "new creature" in Christ and as 2 Corinthians 5:17 says, "..old things are passed away; behold, all things are become new." All of Heaven is celebrating! You have a brand new life with Jesus and a bright future filled with faith and hope.

Waterfall- a fall or perpendicular descent of a stream of water. Thus does Webster's Dictionary give the definition. In this book you will find each waterfall with its official name and or unofficial name that's been given to name the falls. All names have come from the park they reside in, topographical maps, stream names, or if nothing else is reliable the name of the street the falls are on. The waterfalls found in Indiana come in a variety of shapes and sizes. From the smallest step in the stream to the largest plunge found in Hanover, from the thinnest trickle of water to a raging torrent, viewing these falls can be a pleasure to be had. Indiana's waterfalls come in many shapes and appearances. Each picture listed below will show a sample of the types of waterfall forms that are found in Indiana with their explanation of each.

One of the more familiar types is the plunge or drop waterfall. This is where a plume of water falls freely through the air before striking the base of the rock below. Shown to the left is Overhang Falls.

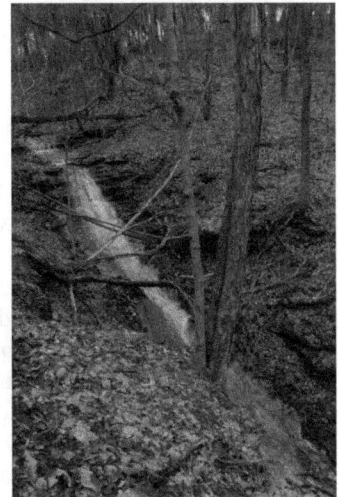

Then we move on to what is referred to as a
Ramp waterfall. This is where water slides down a steeply inclined rock
face without ever losing contact with the rock surface. This is London Road Falls to the right.

Similar to the ramp is the cascade waterfall. This is a common waterfall found in Indiana. Water descends over the rock in many breaks, leaps and small tiers. Brushy Creek Falls, to the left, is one example of the many cascades found around Madison.

Tina Karle

The next class of waterfall almost resembles the ramp waterfall but is slightly different. Water flows across a smooth inclined rock face. This is a slide waterfall. County Road 275 is an example of the slide falls.

The tiered waterfall, as shown below, descends from a series of several falls, with at least two of the waterfalls being seen from one vantage point. This is Indian Kentuck Cemetery Falls.

These are just a general listing of some of the types of waterfalls to be found in Indiana. Some waterfalls make up more than one of the above listed types. In this book you will find many unique characteristics to the waterfalls. Each set of falls is unique to its own self and many change colors as the season's progress. From summers deep green colors and waters muted flow, to fall with colorful swirling leaves that eddy and swirl in the churning waters or being plastered flat to the moist rock surface, they add an enchanting rainbow of color to the falls. Ah but come winter part of the water stops and stands still for a little while and you can see the pale greens and arctic blue's in the face of the frozen falls. Springs thaw brings rampaging muddy waters with hues of a brilliant green surrounding the murky waters. Waterfalls, they each have their own personality to enjoy. So come out and visit these marvelous wonders that God has created for all of us to enjoy.

Note:
There are **no maps** listed in this book. If one would wish to have a map of the hike you are about to take, please refer to mapquest.com, mytopo.com, or topomaker.com to print out a handy map of the surrounding area. These can come in handy for directions, names of creeks otherwise not mentioned, rest areas, side streets, and just a general idea of where you are going!

Introduction

The first documented European visit came on May 23, 1791 when General Charles Scott and a mounted company of 852 men crossed the river five miles below the mouth of the Kentucky River at Battle Creek, which may have been an older name for the Indian-Kentuck Creek. A 1925 article by J.W. Whickour, based on contemporary accounts, says the company marched through Switzerland, Jefferson, Jennings, and other counties on their way to Indian villages on the Wabash. In 1793, two teenagers, John and Peter Smock, were captured by Indians in Shelby Co., Ky. An 1874 account by their nephew John Smock says that pursuers trailed the Indians to the Ohio River. The Indians cross the river at Clifty Creek and stayed for three days on the present courthouse site. Madison is over 200 years old. As far as is known the first non-Native American cabin was built in Madison about May 30, 1808. In 1810 Jonathan Lyon, with John Paul and Lewis Davis, laid out the town. The first sale of lots was in 1811. Situated on the Ohio across from Kentucky, the settlement was a favored and inviting spot for commerce and industry and it grew rapidly. It was incorporated as a town April 15, 1824, as a city by the act of Legislature of 1838. Madison was a place of much note at the early part of last century. A great number of people of all classes, characters and occupations came to it. In 1816 and up to 1850, it was one of the points of attraction as a new and growing town in a new and growing country .Today the pleasant thriving city that nestles amid the hills of Jefferson County is one of the most picturesque and beautiful spots in the state. It has an ancient lore combined with a modern progress that makes it attractive to all who have an eye for the beautiful in scenery or a mind for the history of the achievements of the past. Madison has a geographical location that is as outstanding as its scenic setting. On the north bank of the Ohio River, approximately 50 miles from Louisville and 75 miles from Cincinnati, it at one time shared with both in commercial and cultural leadership. With the building of the first railroad in the United States, west of the Allegheny Mountains, from Madison to Indianapolis, Madison became the gateway to the settlement of the vast Northwest Territory. Creek and stayed for three days on the present courthouse site.

The early industries of Madison included some of the following: Ship yards, starch factories, furniture factory, saw mills, cotton mills, button factories, paper mill, yarn and cordage mill, breweries, pork packing industries, and iron foundries. The two latter played an important part in the history of the town. But with the pork industries moving away, the growth of Madison stopped.

During the 1840's Madison was the only city in this part of the country with a railroad. By 1835 the Michigan Road extended through to the Great Lakes and various roads spreading out in different directions. This time Madison was the greatest "porkopolis" in the world, Chicago having not stolen her franchise on the great industry of the West. Hogs were sent to Madison by car load and wagon load. Hundreds of thousands of hogs arrived here on foot, having traveled great distances from surrounding states. Madison was the second pork packing city in the west and the new rail- road did a big business hauling hogs during the winter months. In the year 1852 they handled 124,000 hogs. The hog trade was the main traffic and there were so few coaches that the railroad was forced to use the hog cars for passengers by making seats in them of clean lumber.

The Schroeder Saddletree Company, maker of fine quality saddletrees. Was in operation from 1850 to 1971. The plant is located on Milton Street between Mulberry and Jefferson Streets and their products were sold to all 50 states as well as practically every South American country .During its long life the plant supplied saddletrees for the Civil War, Spanish-American War, Boer War, First World War and Second World War. The building is now owned by Historic Madison. The organization plans to restore the building and open it to the public.

In 1870, there were several iron foundries in Madison. They furnished most of the old gates, fences and balconies in use today. However, the balconies on the Lanier House were imported. Much of the iron work seen in New Orleans was made in Madison. The beautiful wrought iron balcony is on the John T. Windle building at 306 West Main Street. The balcony extends in front of long windows across the second story of a three story brick building. The intricate detail woven into the unusual lyre pattern of the balcony makes it an outstanding example of wrought iron work.

Tina Karle

The first newspaper, "Western Eagle", was published in Madison. It was owned by Colonel John Paul and published by his son-in-law, William Hendricks. The first issue was dated May 26, 1813, Madison, Ind. Territory. The Madison Courier was published as a weekly in 1837. In 1849 it was changed to a daily publication and purchased by Michael C. Garber. In 1937 the paper celebrated its centennial year, and in 1949 observed its hundredth year as a daily, and also its hundred years under management of one family. It is now the second oldest newspaper in Indiana, (the Vincennes Sun is older) and the only one to have been owned for over a hundred years by the same family.

The Jefferson County Jail was just a building for the imprisonment of town drunks and petty thieves; but more looking like a medieval dungeon with its stone walls two feet thick, reinforced with cannon balls and its windowless cells just large enough to hold a single cot. Built in 1849, the key to the outer door measuring at least twelve inches in length was handed to the County Commissioners in an elaborate ceremony. In 1878 when John Beaver was hanged in the Courthouse yard for murder, people gathered for miles around, standing on roof tops and in available space to see the first and only hanging in Jefferson County. Many brought lunch boxes crammed with good things to eat and it was evidently a gala occasion for everyone but poor Mr. Beaver. The jail is an interesting land mark. It was remodeled in 1960 and is still in use. The heavy cornices and well designed window caps on the upper portions of the store fronts on both sides of Main Street were made to resemble carved stone. They date from the 1850's and 1860's and show the influence of the Italian Villa style of architecture which was so popular over the country at that time. Main Street, Madison possesses some very fine examples of this style. In the year 1831, a Volunteer Fire Fighters Club was organized in Madison. Their headquarters and meeting place was a small one room frame building on the corner of Main and Walnut Streets, the present site of the Soldiers and Sailors monument. As the city grew, so grew the Volunteer Fire Fighters and on September 15, 1841 the organization set up a Constitution, changing the company's name to "Fair Play Fire Company Number One". A charter was granted for the same on September 6, 1849. This company, being the oldest volunteer fire company in the state of Indiana, first saw action as a "Bucket Brigade". The company then purchased a hand drawn piece of fire equipment in 1851. It was called "Neptune" and had to be pulled to all fires by its members with the aid of a long rope. It is still in the possession of the fire company. On April 3, 1888 the Company purchased their present home located at the N. E. corner of Main and Walnut Streets. The first meeting was held on October 1, 1888. In 1871 the Fair Play Company purchased the first steam engine (horse drawn) manufactured by Chris Ahrens. On September 15, 1886 the Company participated in a Fireman's Tournament, held at Cincinnati, Ohio and walked away with first prize for throwing water the farthest distance. The prize was $400.00. As the city of Madison grew, new companies were organized and at the present time Madison is fortunate enough to have six volunteer fire departments. Each company has its own constitution and by-laws, its own officers and owns all of its equipment. The total cost to the city of Madison is far less than one paid fire department would cost. Madison also is one of the few cities that still have approximately 35 cisterns in which water is stored as a sort of reservoir, for use in fighting fires. These cisterns are filled from the city water system and at times of fires valves are turned on to furnish plenty of water. Listed below are names of cities, villages and or townships that have waterfalls in them surrounding the city of Madison.

Bryantsburg is an unincorporated town in Monroe Township, Jefferson County, Indiana. Bryantsburg was platted on March 5, 1834, by Jacob Bryant with 32 lots. The Bryantsburg Presbyterian Church was formed by Sept. 22, 1854 when the trustees of the parent Monroe Presbyterian Church sold land to the Bryantsburg Trustees. The deed mentions a lot on which the Bryantsburg Church "now stands." The 1855 and 1857 minutes of the General Assembly of the Presbyterian Church in the U.S.A. reported Bryantsburg had 20 communicants. Fifteen were listed in the 1862 and 1863 minutes. Its operation had probably ended by April 30, 1867 when the church trustees sold the lot and meeting house. The town existed on both sides of the Michigan Road (U.S. 421), but the west portion, which was the biggest section, became part of the former

Jefferson Proving Ground in 1941, leaving a handful of houses on the east side. According to a history of schools compiled just after the government had taken the land, the Bryantsburg School opened in 1822 as a subscription school and closed on March 7, 1941. It was located about a mile north of Bryantsburg on the west side of the Michigan Road.

The town was described this way in an 1889 history: "Bryantsburg: Monroe township was laid off by Jacob Bryant, March 5th, 1834. It contains a post-office, three stores, and two blacksmith shops. It has a population of about 60. It is in section eleven, town V, range X east."

Canaan began growing slowly with the establishment of John Warfield's farm in 1812. The first known use of the name Canaan is dated November 15, 1832 when Edwards Ayres advertised that he had opened the Bee Hive, a public house, 14 miles from Canaan and 12 miles from Madison. On May 6, 1833 a road petition mentions Canaan in renaming a road to Versailles, Indiana beginning at Canaan. It is generally recognized that Amos Simpers founded Canaan by virtue of the fact that he sold 7 lots laid out along the road that is now State Road 62. During the 1840s and 1850s a number of people operated businesses within the area of Canaan. In 1829 a tavern was established by E.B. Bishop and a man by the last name of Etherton. In 1837 Ephraim and Coy Kennedy opened a store and by 1840 they were operating Kennedy & Bros., a tobacco factory employing 7 people. By 1850, 8000 pounds of tobacco was used in the production of cigars in which case 780,00 were produced in 1850 and 750,000 were produced in 1870. By 1878, Canaan would also have a drug store. The existence of businesses other than stores and the carding mill have little documentation before 1850. The late Alois Bishop reported that Etherton & Littlejohn briefly operated a tavern near the site of the former Bishop feed mill in1829. Perhaps Littlejohn is related was related to Jared Littlejohn, age 33, listed on the 1850 census for Canaan as an Innkeeper. It is not known how long that establishment, or Ayre's Bee Hive, operated.

China is an unincorporated community in Shelby Township, Jefferson County, Indiana. It spans Shelby and Madison Townships and was for years largely defined by the existence of a general store in Madison Township and the former St. Anthony's Catholic Church in Shelby Township. Razor's Fork runs between the two sections. Indiana State Road 62 runs parallel to Razor's Fork in Madison Township, and then crosses the stream and heads north to Canaan. The origin of the name is not known. In her history of St. Anthony's Church, area resident Elma related a story, which she said was confirmed by Catholic priests, that China stemmed from the name of Father Munnschina, a priest. In the late 1960s, Mrs. Frances Ringwald, whose daughter Edith and son William "Bud" Thomas, operated the China store, said she was told that the site had mulberry trees, which suggested silk, which suggested China. However, China post office opened on January 30, 1833 and closed on November 29, 1838 and that was years before the arrival of the German Catholics who founded St. Anthony's and who were served by Munnschina. In fact, the first China post master was Moses Wilder, who was a Presbyterian Minister had arrived in nearby Madison, by 1830, as an agent of the American Tract Society. Wilder may have been associated with the Center or Central (Presbyterian records use both names) Presbyterian Church was founded by Feb. 4, 1833 when deeds from two families transferred land to church trustees. The site was on the east side of the West Fork of the Indian-Kentuck creek and on the north side of Dry Fork at their meeting. Minutes of the General Assembly of the Presbyterian Church in the U.S.A. showed 36 communicants in 1834. Minutes are unclear as to whether it lasted to 1852 since in 1851 and 1852, the church issued no record and prior member records were reiterated. A paper mill, which operated as the China Paper mill, was located near the church site. It may have been founded by Samuel Demaree who died in 1826. A local history indicates two of his sons-in-law, James Hamilton and Henry Jackman. They sold the property Demaree's grandsons, William U. and Samuel B. Demaree, with the 1850 U.S. Census of Manufacturers listing W&S Demaree as a paper maker. They sold the mill property to Henry James on June 4, 1855 and he sold it back to the Demarees in 1860, with the mill's engine sold off.

After German Catholics began arrive in the mid-1840s, St. Anthony's was founded. In his history, William J. Kremer says that the first Mass was read on St. Anthony's Day, June 13, 1849, in a brick house the farm home of Hans Weber. The farm house was described by a tornado in 1974. Land for the church building was sold to the Bishop of Vincennes on April 15, 1851.Records of the Diocese of Indianapolis show that a log church was erected in 1861 on the south section of the present building with the sandstone church building that is still standing, constructed in 1869. The church operated until 1993, when it was made part of the combined Prince of Peace Parish. It is now owned by a Catholic retreat, which offers masses and which also operates a religious store in the garage of the former China store.

East Enterprise, village in Switzerland County. Formerly called Clapboard Corner, for a clapboard mill here. A post office was established in 1823 as Allensville, and the name was changed to East Enterprise in 1964. The present name in commendatory.

Friendship, village in Ripley County. Laid out in 1849 by William Hart and originally called Hart's Mills. In 1870 the postmaster changed the name to Friendship "because most of the people were friendly."

Hanover-Captain George Logan (1780-May 12, 1875) grew up in a farming household in the area of Lexington, Kentucky. In the late winter of 1801, young Logan loaded a barge with produce and embarked on a journey westward on the Ohio River, ultimately to sell the produce in New Orleans. At the time, he later noted, there were no European settlements in the area between present-day Carrollton, Kentucky and Louisville. According to Logan, both banks of the river were covered in thick forest. He also reported seeing Native American hunters and fishermen, a large number of buffalo and deer, and heard the cries of coyotes. Faced with heavy winds and harsh weather towards the end of February, Logan was forced to stop his procession. He stopped his barge roughly a half mile west of the present-day area of Hanover Beach. After waiting for several days, he reportedly grew bored and decided to head ashore. Present-day Hanover is located on a hill overlooking the river valley below. Armed with a rifle, Logan decided to explore and he climbed this hill to the spot today known as Logan's Point. This was the first recorded instance of a European exploring the area of Hanover. Logan was so enamored with the view from atop Logan's Point that he resolved he would some day move there. He carved his initials on a beech tree along with the date, March 1, 1801. It would be another fourteen years before he would return to settle permanently. Judge Williamson Dunn (December 25, 1781-November 11, 1854), from Mercer County, Kentucky, was 27 when, on November 28, 1808, he purchased the land area of modern Hanover from the federal government. The following year, in 1809, Dunn resettled his entire family to the area, and they became the first residents of a town called "Dunn's Settlement," which would later come to be known as Hanover. A steady flow of settlers then followed, most of whom were Scotch-Irish Presbyterians. These early settlers had largely emigrated from Ireland to Virginia, then to Kentucky, and finally to the area of Hanover Among these early settlers in Dunn's Settlement was Christopher Harrison (1780–1868), who would later serve as Indiana's first lieutenant governor and would play a key role in the planning of the state capital in Indianapolis. Harrison built a homestead at Logan's Point, the very spot where George Logan had hoped to build a home years before. When in 1815 Logan returned to attempt to find the spot that he had marked in 1801, the two men met. Logan bought the land and settled there permanently, while Harrison moved to Salem, Indiana. The next year he would be elected as lieutenant governor. Although most of the fledgling town's population was Presbyterian, initially the nearest church was located in Charlestown, Indiana, 25 miles to the west. On March 4, 1820, Searle founded the Hanover Presbyterian Church. His wife, a native of Hanover, New Hampshire, was greatly admired by the church's congregants; therefore, the church adopted the name it did. Before long, the town also adopted the name "Hanover," although officially it could only be named "South Hanover" because a post office was already in existence in Shelby County for a town of "Hanover." When the other town of Hanover ceased to support a post office, then South Hanover's name was shortened to Hanover. Founding of Hanover College. John Finley Crowe, founder of Hanover College John Finley Crowe (June 16, 1787-January 17, 1860) was born in Greene County, Tennessee and grew up in Tennessee and Missouri. He grew up in a Presbyterian household, although he was not terribly religious. However, after meeting some Presbyterian elders who had moved from North Carolina to his area in Missouri, Crowe became interested in pursuing a religious education. He attended Transylvania College in Lexington, Kentucky, and then continued his education at Princeton Theological Seminary in Princeton, New Jersey. After completing his Masters of Divinity in 1815, Crowe accepted his first ministerial assignment in

Shelbyville, Kentucky. While there, Crowe became actively involved in the abolitionist movement. He established a Sunday School for African-American children, although he could not find a location in the area that would permit such a school to meet. On May 7, 1822, he began publication of the *Abolition Intelligence and Missionary Magazine*. Crowe's abolitionist sympathies alienated him from his slave-holding neighbors, and it was not long before he lost access to the printing press. On April 2, 1823, John M. Dickey, moderator of a church session that also seated Williamson Dunn and George Logan as elders, sent a letter to Crowe inviting him to serve at the Hanover Presbyterian Church. Sickened by the increasingly hostile attitude of his neighbors in Kentucky towards his abolitionist views, Crowe accepted the position, relieved to move to a state where the possession of slaves was illegal. Shortly after his arrival in Hanover, Crowe began construction of a residence, known today as the Crowe-Garritt House. Located just north of the present-day Hanover Presbyterian Church, the Crowe-Garritt House was added to the National Register of Historical Places in 1980.

Not long after his arrival at the Hanover Presbyterian Church, Crowe began petitioning church members to sponsor the founding of a seminary. While congregants were reluctant at first to take on the task, ultimately he prevailed, and a religious school opened in Hanover on January 1, 1827. Initially, classes met in the Presbyterian Church's old stone church building, which was located in the present-day area of the Hanover Firehouse. Within a year, donated land for the construction of a new college edifice. In 1829, the state of Indiana granted a charter for a Hanover Academy, while the Presbyterian Synod of Indiana recognized the theological segment of the school as the Indiana Seminary. While the Hanover Academy grew exponentially over the ensuing years, the seminary stagnated; the two entities split in 1836, and in 1841 the seminary moved to New Albany, Indiana. Ultimately, faced with money problems and a split amongst students on the issue of slavery, in 1859 the seminary once again moved, this time reopening as McCormick Theological Seminary in Chicago, Illinois. Meanwhile, the Hanover Academy in 1833 received a charter from the state of Indiana to form a college by the name of Hanover College.

Jefferson Proving Ground-The history of the proving ground dates to 1940, when the Army came to southeastern Indiana and purchased approximately 400-500 homes and farms for creating a military base with the purpose of munitions testing. According to Ken Knouf, the Army's civilian director at JPG, residents in the area purchased were given just a little more than a month to pack their belongings and vacate their homes. Then on the verge of entering World War II, the military moved quickly to prepare the area and fired the first round of ammunition just five months later, in May 1941. That round was just the beginning of six decades of munitions testing at the site. During times of peak testing at the facility, Knouf said, rounds were fired 24 hours a day, seven days a week, with blasting so loud that at times it shattered the windows of nearby homes. Over nearly 55 years of operation, JPG tested ammunition during four wars, including World War II, the Korean Conflict, the Vietnam and Persian Gulf wars. When the country wasn't at war, the base would enter what Knouf called "caretaker" status, and by the late 1980s, government officials decided to close the base. In 1989, JPG became part of what the U.S. Department of Defense called the Base Realignment and Closure program. Under the program, bases that were identified as no longer necessary were closed and the land and facilities transferred, where possible, to civilian use. Unfortunately, in the case of JPG, the 51,000 acres north of the firing line were contaminated and could not be released. The Army retained ownership of that area and in 1997 agreed to allow the U.S. Fish and Wildlife Service to manage the land's ecosystem. In 2000, the Big Oaks National Wildlife Refuge was created as an overlay refuge. Additionally, in 1998 Army officials agreed to allow the

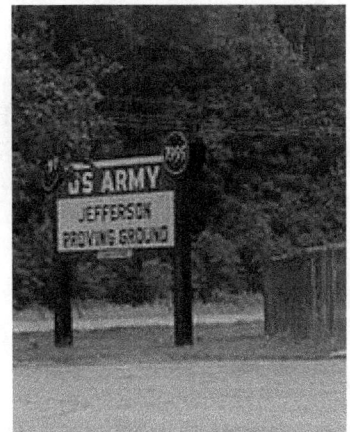

15

Tina Karle

Indiana Air National Guard to use 1,033 acres north of the firing line for air-to-ground training. Today, about 30,000 are completely closed to access, due to possible hazards from contamination. "Some of the areas are really dangerous," Knouf said. "We don't even go into those areas." He said those areas will probably never be accessible because of the major cost of cleanup, estimated to be more than $1 billion. Nearly 4,000 acres south of the firing line, however, became available in 1995. Robert Hudson, who worked for 34 years at JPG as the civilian technical director, was appointed as the base transition coordinator. In this position, Hudson worked as a liaison between the federal and local government in the transfer of the property. Hudson said one goal of the process was to transfer federal property to local communities for use in creating new jobs to replace the ones lost by the closure of the base. In order for communities to acquire property, such as JPG, from the federal government, an application detailing how the property would be managed had to be submitted. Hudson said that Madison submitted such a plan and that he attended the meeting in Washington, D.C., where the plan was evaluated.

But due to technical problems with the application, Madison's plan was denied, and JPG slipped from the community's grasp. Defense Department officials instead decided to auction the property in September 1995, but no one stepped forward to meet the required minimum bid of $6 million. A second auction was held in December, when Ford decided to take advantage of the opportunity.

Although Ford had been active in buying farms and other properties in the past, he admitted that acquiring JPG occurred "strictly by accident." Ford said that what started out as joke with a friend about bidding on the property ended up a serious proposition when he saw the bid packet. Ford's friend, John Harrell, had sent off for an auction information packet, something Ford said he never would have done, and brought it by for him to see. When Ford saw the details, a deal that originally seemed "too big" for him suddenly became quite reasonable. The only question left in Ford's mind was how much to bid.

A caveat of the auction was that the Army would only accept a bid that they considered fair. In order to determine what that might be, Ford's wife, Debbie, set off for the library, where she found a book, "For Defense of Our Country, Echoes of Jefferson Proving Ground," by Sue Baker. In the book, Baker details the Army's cost to build JPG, including land, roads and walks, permanent buildings and sewers and water lines. Ford said he used the information in Baker's book to determine his bid. Ford entered a sealed bid of $5.1 million at the auction, held at the U.S. Army Corps of Engineers' office in Louisville. His winning bid for the 3,400 acres south of the firing line went down in history, since JPG earned the distinction of becoming the only installation in the Base Realignment and Closure program to be owned by a private individual rather than a community. Although Ford's purchase created some controversy in the community, Madison Mayor Al Huntington said he is pleased with the number of jobs that have been created through the location of businesses at JPG. "The Jefferson Proving Ground offers a tremendous span of land that is ideally suited for industrial, commercial or recreational development, and I am excited about the opportunities it offers for the entire Madison-Jefferson County area," said Huntington.

For Ford, fulfilling a childhood dream is only part of the appeal of owning a piece of JPG. It has also been a successful business venture. Because of environmental issues, the land is being released to Ford in parcels. So far, two parcels have been released to Ford. He expects a third to be released in January. Ford currently leases about 13 buildings, 38 residences, and about 800 acres for farming on the property. Additionally, Ford has sold for $1.3 million a 34-acre tract to the State of Indiana to build a state highway garage.

North Vernon, fifth class city in Jennings County. Platted in 1854 north of the older town of Vernon; hence, the name is locational.

Olean, village in Ripley County. Laid out in 1857 and named for Olean, New York, home of settlers.

Patriot, town in Switzerland County. Laid out in 1820 and named Troy, for Troy, New York. The present name is inspirational. One local anecdote says the name comes form "the Patriots," veterans of the Revolution who settled here, while a more likely account says that when the name was changed form Troy, town leaders wanted to rename the town Washington for the greatest patriot, but since there already were several towns of that name in Indiana, they settled for Patriot.

16

Quercus Grove, village in Switzerland County. Sometimes called Bark Works, the town was settled in 1816 by Daniel D. Smith and others, who ground and packed oak bark to send to England for dyes, hence the name Quercus Grove, i.e., "Oak Grove."

Rising Sun, county seat, fifth class city in Ohio County. Platted in 1814. "The name was suggested by the grandeur of the sunrise over the Kentucky hills above the town of Rabbit Hash across the river." Local legend offers another explanation: "That's how Rising Sun got its name. They was going down the river [Ohio River], and the sun was a comin` up, an` they said, `look at the rising sun.` And that's right about along where Rising Sun is, an` that's how they named it. The Indians give Rising Sun its name."

Saluda, village in Jefferson County. A post office was established in 1828. Named for Saluda Township, in which it is located. The name appears in other states and originally was an Indian name applied to a river and meaning "river of corn."

Vernon-Bordered on three sides by the winding waters of a river called the Muscatatuck, this little Southeastern Indiana town maintains a rich and distinguished heritage. Vernon was founded in 1815 by Col. John Vawter, a United States surveyor who surely knew a good spot for a town when he saw one. From the beginning, Vernon was a planned community, as John Vawter's detailed plat set aside spaces for schools, churches and recreation. This was possibly the first town in American history in which a portion of the proceeds from each lot sold was used to finance the county library. Vernon can claim many firsts. The elevated railroad and underpass, known locally as "the culvert", were the first west of the Alleghenies and are still in use. It also was the first Indiana town, thanks to Vawter's plat, to have a public playground. This green field on the Muscatatuck's banks was called "the commons" and is today a popular spot for watching the annual canoe race. Vernonites have a tradition of doing things differently. Like Hickman New, they go against the grain. In 1851, Vernon adopted a unique town charter that still has them holding elections unlike any others in the state. Indiana law says that towns under 2,000 cannot elect a mayor. Vernon, population 170, does anyway. The charter requires an elected mayor with a two-year term; every other mayor in Indiana serves for four. There are no partisan restrictions, no primaries. To run for office in Vernon, you need only toss your hat in the ring. This is almost literally the case, as Baron Wilder, the current mayor, found out when he first came to the county courthouse in Vernon and asked how the town election process worked. "Put your name in the tin can," he was told. Attempts to abolish the 1851 charter were made in the 19th and early 20th centuries, mostly by those who also wanted to move the Jenning's county seat from Vernon to North Vernon. But the town fought back hard, and in 1948 the Indiana Supreme Court ruled that Vernon, the smallest county seat in the entire state, would be able to keep the authority of its courthouse and the quirky requirements of its 1851 charter intact. During the Civil War era, the people of this town fought against another injustice- slavery. Vernon was an important stop along the Underground Railroad. Citizens sheltered escaping slaves and aided them in their flight north to freedom. For the Confederates, though, Vernon was the northernmost point reached in Indiana. On July 11th, 1863, Gen. John Hunt Morgan and his raiders approached the town from the south, demanding its surrender. The demand was refused. Morgan, wrongly thinking himself to be outnumbered, turned away and continued his raid into Ohio, where he was ultimately captured. In 1976, Vernon, Indiana was added in its entirety to the National Register of Historic Places. With a stately courthouse square, streets lined with old homesteads, scenic river bends where the outcropped ruins of Tunnel and Vinegar Mill mingle with the bluebells, Vernon certainly deserves outside recognition. But the town that founder John Vawter named after the home of George Washington was designed to be self-reliant. Its citizens honor their heritage by continuing to be the same stubbornly independent thinkers they have always been. You have to admire a community that refuses to make any amendments to their 1851 Charter-- the one giving their town marshal sole responsibility for "seizing and impounding wild hogs, suppressing riots and rounding up unruly chickens and ducks."

Tina Karle

Versailles-county seat, town in Ripley County. Founded in 1818 and named for the French town and palace. During the Civil War, Morgan's Raiders made their way through the area that is now the park. The town of Versailles was briefly under Confederate control. This area has deep history rooted in both the Civil War and the Civilian Conservation Corps.

Vevay, county seat, town in Switzerland County. Founded in 1802 by Swiss settlers, platted in1813, and named for the commune in Switzerland. When John James Dufour, a Swiss immigrant fleeing Napoleon's armies, set foot in America in 1796, there was no American wine industry. He had been sent by his family to scout the best possible place to start a Swiss colony devoted to wine making. He traveled through the Mid Atlantic states and found nothing that represented a successful vineyard. He then crossed the Appalachian Mountains, descended the Ohio River and eventually settled near Lexington, Kentucky where he founded a vineyard funded by the sale of shares to the wealthy citizens of that city. Dufour planted the vineyard in 1799 with mostly European varieties. The vines grew well for a couple of years, but soon failed, following the same path of decline that others had witnessed over the past two centuries. Despite the failure, he noticed that one variety, the Cape, seemed to do better than all the others. When the investors lost interest, Dufour sought out a new sight for the Swiss colony that was on its way from Europe. He purchased land in the newly surveyed Indiana Territory north of the Ohio River. He took cuttings of the Cape grape to plant at the new site that would later become Vevay, Indiana. The Cape grapes planted at Vevay proved to be the basis for the first successful wine production in the United States. Today we know why the Cape was successful. It was not a true European variety, but a cross of a wild native grape and a European grape; making it hardy enough to survive in North America while also exhibiting useful wine making characteristics. In the late 1800's and early 1900's wineries dotted the Indiana countryside. Indiana was the tenth largest grape producing state in the country until Prohibition. Today the Indiana wine industry is once again thriving.

The keys listed on this page are a guide to help you understand the terminology used in this book under the descriptions of the hikes and falls themselves.

Form:
Drop/Plunge: Descends straight down, has no contact with the rock
Cascade: Small falls made up of a large near vertical drop of water
        hitting the rocks continuously in a stair step fashion.
Tiered: A large waterfall that is broken up into 2 or more separate
        falls that is seen from one vantage point.
Slide: Water drops down a smooth angled rock face.

Access:
This is the rating for the hike based on how much stamina/energy is required to walk the hike.

Easy: Simple to walk, not much effort required. Trail is generally
        flat with few hills.
Moderate: Some steep inclines or hills to be hiked as well as
        possible steps. You can become winded and may need
        an occasional rest. Some off trail hiking is possible as
        well.
Hard: You will have a work out! Steep hills, sometimes no trail,
        general bushwhacking through high weeds, low level of
        tree and rock bouldering, sometimes trail is the creek
        itself leading to the falls and water shoes/boots are
        required. Rest breaks will be a must!

Coordinates:
For those who have a GPS (global positioning satellite) unit, these are the latitude/longitude numbers given for the falls. Most readings were done either on top of the waterfall, the parking lot, roadside, or end of trail areas. **Coordinates are done in degree/minutes and decimal minutes. D/Min.MM** They will appear in the book like this: 29.56.34N 84.45.84W. The period is there as a spacer between the numbers as I do not have the correct symbols to use next to the numbers. Some hikes listed in this book can only be done using the GPS unit, as they require heavy off trail or no trail usage. Using the GPS helps guide the user safely to and back in no trail circumstances. Hence the limited information about the hike. Also, you can go online and convert these coordinates to any coordinate you feel more comfortable using for your GPS unit. IE: degrees decimal minutes

Height:
Most all of the taller waterfalls have been measured for better accuracy on the true height of the falls. Medium to small falls have estimated heights.

Water:
Stream flow at a waterfall is determined by two factors: size of the watershed and recent precipitation history. A watershed is defined as the area whose runoff can flow to a given location. The larger the watershed the longer time period of water flows. In smaller watershed area's to see the falls run, attention must be given to weather conditions. These are best seen right after a rain in general. Definitions for the seasons are provided below.

Tina Karle

Spring: Weather is generally still cool. Rainy conditions, flowers
         and new greenery, melting snow, provides better water flow.

Summer: Generally hot and humid, less water flow, weeds are
         more prominate, some falls are harder to see due to
         deeper green foliage. Snakes are more active.
Fall: Temperature is moderate to cool at night, low water flow
         is not uncommon, foliage becomes a brilliant background of
         bright colors.
Winter: Cold temperatures and less daylight, during colder temps
         low water flow can produce beautiful ice formations.
         Moderate flows are possible as well due to snow melt or
         rainfall. Trees are a dull brown in color, no foliage is
         visible, falls are easier to spot.
Year: Water has a year round flow. Large creeks, rivers, and springs tend to
         run year round.

Distance:
Estimated distance from vehicle to the best view of the falls. Some of the hikes only have the city listed. For example Old Mill Road Falls has Rock Way, Ohio as the directions. Hikes that have only the city mentioned are harder hikes, have no trails, require a lot of wisdom, and usually are steep rough hikes that require a lot of climbing or scrambling over fallen objects. These are just GPS only hikes for that reason. Generally are not for an afternoon stroll through the park type of hike!

Bench:
This refers to a resting place, to get off of one's feet, or a place to relax at the waterfall. They can average from a wooden bench, metal chairs, a rock wall or ledge, a large rock, and or a log or fallen tree. Not all falls have places to sit; this is mentioned for those, which do.

Restrooms:
This is for either a public bathroom, or Porto let or similar type restrooms.

Maps
Again, there are no maps listed for this book. If you would like to use a map to help you in locating the falls listed for this book, you may log onto www.mapquest.com, www.google.com or www.mytopo.com for maps.

Rating System

Numbered Rating- Every waterfall listed in this book has been assigned a rating from one to four. This gives an instant knowing of the scenic value, accessibility, and water flow of the waterfall. This rating system is based on the author's knowledge of the falls.

1. This type of waterfall is located throughout the state of Indiana! Based on the uniqueness of this waterfall one will judge if they wish to visit this hike. Also, a one may be given due to:
a. Low water flow
b. Poor view of the falls
c. Natural or human debris that clogs the falls

2. This waterfall is of a modest scenic value. Additionally a two may be given due to:
a. Ease of seeing the falls
b. Water flow is slightly better and lasts longer than a day
c. Natural or human debris is distracting

3. This waterfall is given a three because of it's scenic worth. This waterfall will be enjoyable to everyone and one would wish to spend time here at this falls. Additional to giving this waterfall a three is:
a. Reasonable water flow: there is a better water source for this waterfall, therefore water flows more often than not.
b. This waterfall has a unique feature to its shape or flow
c. The surrounding scenery compliments the waterfall
d. Lack of a great view all around keeps this from being at a higher rating

4. This waterfall is an outstanding feature. This waterfall varies in size and can be as small as Five feet tall or as large as one hundred feet tall! Other reasons for having labeled this falls a four are:
a. Water flow is almost year round
b. A unique shape or form to the falls
c. The scenery around the falls enhances the beauty of the falls.
d. Perfect view all the way around this waterfall

This rating system sometimes could have different numbers based on the criteria for the falls. Some falls though they may be large, lacks water flow to make them an outstanding feature too visit as you have to catch it running at a certain time. Not all falls are going to meet the criteria for each number and letter for said number. This is just a guide to help you judge, based on the numbers if you wish to visit such a falls.

Before You Begin Your Hike

1. Make sure you are wearing sturdy walking shoes. In some area's wearing waterproof boots are best for traversing through the creeks.

2. Wear comfortable clothing. Wear layers during winter months and remove as needed. Cotton is great to wear during summer months, as it will keep you cooler. Wool or Gortex is great for winter months. Don't forget your umbrella or rain jacket in case of a sudden storm. Watch the weather. Bring along an extra pair of socks or shoes in case of slippery trails, or a sudden tumble.

3. Bring with you fluids to drink along your hike, if you plan to be out all day. A knapsack is handy to have for carrying water and snacks as well as that handy extra pair of socks or gloves! Don't forget to bring along a snack for along the way to keep up your energy on the longer hikes!

4. Have with you or in your car some band aides, washcloth, first aid kit, insect repellant, itch cream, and some aspirin for just such emergencies. The author carries with her a roll of toilet paper as well, for such certain emergencies that can't just wait!

5. Carry with you on your hike, if you so choose, a handy compass, food, water, map, umbrella, knapsack that can hold such items as well as a knife, hat, bandanna, GPS unit, and dry clothing. But this is up to each individual as to what they wish to carry.

6. To print out a handy topography or street map of the selected hike get on topozone.com, topomaker.com, and or mapquest.com. This will help you have an idea of where certain roads or creeks are located on the hike. The GPS coordinates are listed for almost every hike except otherwise noted.

7. Last but not least don't forget your camera, or video camera to record for posterity your memorial visit to such beautiful places.

Authors Note

This book is to be used as a guide for finding and locating the waterfalls in and around Madison Indiana. Madison has a weather pattern that is diverse and makes photographing the waterfalls in and around this area a challenge due to the constant change in weather. There are many diverse waterfalls in and around Madison Indiana. Though some of the falls may not be large in stature and to some may be yawn inspiring, to others they are unique treasures each in their own right to be found and enjoyed. Some locations of the waterfalls are in quiet woodlands where you can walk and stop and enjoy the sound of nature in the heart of a busy and thriving city. This book is for the book reader who wants to take a minute and stop and enjoy the small bit of nature that surrounds each set of different and interesting falls. I am not claiming to be a fantastic photographer but I try to include decent pictures of each waterfall. I include several photographs for each waterfall if time allows to show the seasons for each set of falls. Time of course is of the essence for all people, likewise for me as well. I am trying to provide a decent book for all to enjoy.

Tina Karle

Aberdeen Road Falls

Rating 3

See, I am sending an angel ahead of you to guard you along the way and to bring you to the place I have prepared. Exodus 23:20

Height: 3 Feet	Restrooms: No
Water: Spring/Winter	Access: Moderate
Form: Cascade	Distance: 1500 Feet
Coordinates: 38.54.28 N 85.06.35 W	Bench: No

Trail

From the edge of the road walk through the brush towards the creek. Walk slightly upstream to the side tributary. Here you will find the lovely set of falls that run fantastic after a good rain!

Directions

From downtown Vevay Indiana, turn right onto Route 56. Follow Route 56 for 5.2 miles. Turn left onto Fairview Road and drive 4.4 miles. Turn left at Route 250 and drive less than 341 feet to turn right onto Bear Branch Road. Drive 2.1 miles and continue onto Milton Bear Branch Road. Turn left at Aberdeen Road and drive two miles. Pull over onto the verge of the road to see this nice set of falls.

Alcove Falls

Rating 4

You are the rock where I am safe. You are my shield, my powerful weapon, and my place of shelter. You rescue me and keep me from being hurt. 2 Samuel 22:3

Height: 10 Feet	Restrooms: No
Water: Spring/Winter	Access: Easy
Form: Drop	Distance: Roadside
Coordinates: 38.54.22 N 85.20.76 W	Bench: No

Trail
From the edge of the road, carefully make your way along the edge of the pool to view this cascading falls. One note of caution, if you decide to get into the lower pool by the road bridge there is heavy silt built up in the base of the pool and you will sink a bit further than you expect.

Directions
From downtown Madison, take US Route 421 going north for 12.4 miles. Turn right onto E Camp Meeting Road and drive 1.2 miles to the falls. Pull off the side of the road so as not to block traffic. The falls cannot be missed as they are directly next to the road.

Dusk   Before all the brush was removed

Winter   Early Spring

Tina Karle

Arnold Creek Falls

Rating 3

At His command the ice melts, the wind blows, and streams begin to flow. Psalms 47:18

Height: 3,4 Feet	Restrooms: No
Water: Year	Access: Moderate
Form: Cascade	Distance: Roadside
Coordinates: 38.55.82 N 84.56.98 W 1st set of falls 38.56.18 N 84.56.02 W last set of falls	Bench: No

There are four sets of falls along Arnold Creek on White Road. The tallest being right next to Palmer Road. It is best to start this hike coming from Cass-Union Road that leads onto White Road. You will see over six waterfalls along this road. At each stop, make your way down the slope to the creeks edge to view each set of falls. There are two other hikes in this book that contain two other hikes that are found along this road. One being Bascom Corner falls and the other are simply called White Road Falls. The first set of falls you encounter, there will be another set shortly downstream and from that one you will see White Road falls across the road.

Directions
In Dillsboro, take Route 262 and head south for 3.3 miles. Turn right to stay on Route 262 and drive another 4.1 miles. Turn right at Cass-Union Road and drive 1.7 miles. Turn left at White Road and drive about 1.5 miles to the first set of falls. Pull off alongside the edge of the road to see the falls.

First set of falls

Downstream a short ways is the 2nd set

Third set of falls

Last and tallest set of falls

Brown Road Falls

Rating 2

But my brothers are as undependable as intermittent streams, as the streams that overflow. When darkened by thawing ice and swollen with melting snow, but that cease to flow in the dry season, and in the heat vanish from their channels. Job 6:15-17

Height: 3 Feet	Restrooms: No
Water: Spring/Winter	Access: Moderate
Form: Cascade	Distance: Roadside
Coordinates: 38.53.38 N 84.56.77 W	Bench: No

Trail
From the edge of the road, you can look over the edge to see these cascading falls that run after a good rain!

Directions
From downtown Vevay take Route 56 going north for 11.3 miles. Turn right onto Route 250 and drive .7 miles. Continue onto Red Hog Pike for .8 miles. Turn left at Upper Grants Creek Road and drive 1.6 miles. Take a slight left onto Brown Road and drive about .2 miles to the cascading falls on your right.

Tina Karle

Brushy Creek Falls

Rating 4

Brush Creek Fish and Wildlife Area was developed in 1964 with land received from the Muscatatuck State Developmental Center (MSDC). Within the property lies the 150-acre Brush Creek Reservoir. The reservoir was constructed in 1953 to provide supplemental water for MSDC and the City of North Vernon.

Height: 15 Feet	Restrooms: No
Water: Spring/Winter	Access: Hard
Form: Tiered	Distance: ¼ Mile
Coordinates: 39.03.49 N 85.31.46 W	Bench: No

Trail

From the gravel parking lot, cross the road and walk across the creek bridge. Look for the faint trail that leads up the slope. Continue to follow this faint path next to the edge and make your way towards the left to traverse down to the side stream coming in from the left. Cross this stream and head towards your right to gain views of this magnificent set of falls! Use caution during high water as the rocks are highly slippery!

Directions

From North Vernon, head east on Route 50 and drive five miles. Turn left onto the road for Muscatatuck School and Brushy Reservoir. Follow this road back and continue to follow to the right around the bend to a four way intersection. Turn left and follow this road for less than .2 of a mile to the next road on your right. Turn right onto this road and once you have crossed the creek bridge pull into the gravel parking area on your right.

Bull Creek Falls

Rating 4

Deck her out in spring showers; fill the God-River with living water. Psalms 65:11

Height: 15 Feet	Restrooms: No
Water: Year	Access: Moderate
Form: Cascade	Distance: Roadside
Coordinates: 38.29.43 N 85.30.09W	Bench: Yes

Trail
The waterfall can be seen from the road, as you are driving around the bend, but if you wish to go closer; park safely off the bend of the road. Walk up the road and climb over the guardrail and walk down the slight hill to the trees. You can carefully pick your way down to the rock overhang and sit on one of the larger rocks to see an uncluttered view of these falls. Care should be taken if visiting after a heavy rain as the falls could be flooded and the current unpredictable.

Directions
From Charlestown, take Route 62 going north. Turn right onto Hibernia Road and proceed about 1.42 miles to a crossway road. Continue going straight, but the road changes names and becomes Blue Ridge Road. Follow for about 1.69 miles and look to your left as you are coming down the hill, to see the falls on your left. Park in a safe, off the side of the road area, if walking over to gain a better view of these lovely falls!

Tina Karle

Butler Falls

Rating 4

Many, O Lord my God, are Your wonderful works which you have done; and your thoughts toward us cannot be recounted to you in order; if I would declare and speak of them, they are more than can be numbered. Psalm 40:5

Height: 5/10/80 Feet	Restrooms: No
Water: Spring/Winter	Access: Hard
Form: Cascade/Drop	Distance: ¼ Mile
Coordinates: 38.42.20 N 85.28.42 W	Bench: No

Trail

From Tull Road, enter the woods and make your way down to the creek. Note the eight foot waterfall to your left. Cross the creek and walk along the edge heading downstream, and note Tull Road Falls, which will be across the creek, ahead of you. Continue down the creek and you will come to a lovely ten foot cascade. Start up the hill, heading away from the creek but continue going downstream; walk over to the overhanging rock. Use caution around this area, as the rock hangs over the edge, and a slip could be fatal. From this vantage point, you get a lovely side view of Butler Falls. Return the way you came.

Directions

From Route 56 in Hanover turn left onto N Main. Go slow past the school zone and turn left onto Tull Road, which is across from the golf course. Park on the verge of the road being cautious not to block traffic.

Upper Falls different views

30

Butler Falls

Ten foot cascade winter

Ten foot falls spring view

Tina Karle

Cali Nature Preserve
Rock Rest Falls

Rating 4

I will open rivers in high places, and fountains in the midst of the valleys: I will make the wilderness a pool of water, and the dry land springs of water. Isaiah 41:18

Height: 15 Feet	Restrooms: No
Water: Spring/Winter	Access: Hard
Form: Plunge	Distance: Roadside
Coordinates: 38.59.67 N 85.36.17 W	Bench: No

Trail

From the pull-off, walk down the road to the drainage ditch trail that leads to the top of the falls. During dry months you can walk across the creek (note the channels in the rock), to the other side of the falls; walk down the hillside at your own risk. Caution should be used if water is high, as a crossing should not be attempted. If the water is high, from the side of the road, take the trail to your left and walk back to the tree with the fallen tree that is sideways for a beautiful view of the entire area. Climb up the hill and return to the pull-off.

Directions

From Route 7 turn left onto Brown Street. Then turn left at the stop sign and drive through the concrete bridge tunnel. Turn right and go over the concrete bridge to the first road on your left. Turn left onto 25E and go exactly one half mile to the pull-off on your left.

Early Spring view of falls

Salamander

Top view of falls

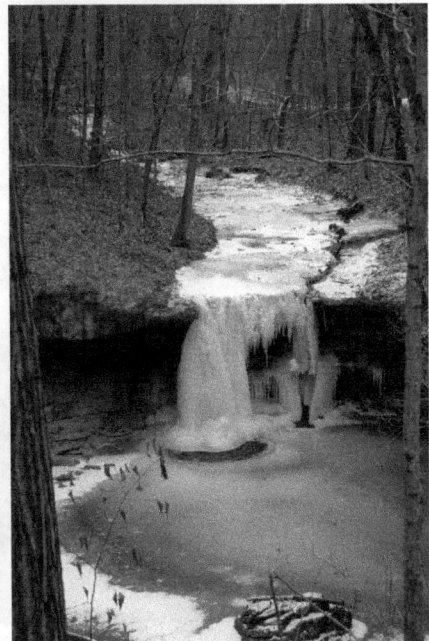

Winter

Tina Karle

Camp Creek Falls

Rating 4

When you pass through the waters, I will be with you; and when you pass through the rivers, they will not sweep over you. When you walk through the fire, you will not be burned; the flames will not set you ablaze. Isaiah 43:2

Height: 6/8 Feet		Restrooms: No	
Water: Year		Access: Easy	
Form: Cascade		Distance: Roadside	
Coordinates: 38.34.23 N 85.29.97 W		Bench: No	

Trail
Walk over to the bridge on the right side to view these pretty falls. Cross the road to the other side watching for traffic and walk to the left side of the bridge to see the other set of falls that cascades next to the concrete bridge.

Directions
From Route 62, near Marysville turn east onto New Washington Bethlehem Road. Follow along the road until you cross Camp Creek. Park by the edge of the bridge.

Winter from the bridge view

Early Spring

Side Falls

Late spring base view

Frontal view

Camp Meeting Road Falls

Rating 4

Streams poured from the rock, flowing like a river! Psalms 78:16

Height: 7 Feet	Restrooms: No
Water: Spring/Winter	Access: Moderate
Form: Cascade	Distance: Roadside
Coordinates: 38.54.23 N 85.20.67 W	Bench: No

Trail
From the edge of the road look for the faint trail which leads into the woods and along the cliff edge. Carefully make your way down the cliff, sometimes sliding down a rock or two and using trees as hand holds; follow the path down to the creeks edge. This is a semi tough hike to the bottom. After a rain it is very slippery so use caution when climbing around the rocks. Also after heavy rains it is best to not try hiking down to the creeks edge as the current is quite dangerous!! Another alternative would be to drive down to where the creek is almost level with the road and hike upstream to the base of the falls if you do not wish to partake of the steep straight climb down.

Directions
From downtown Madison, take US Route 421 going north for 12.4 miles. Turn right onto E Camp Meeting Road and drive 1.48 miles to the falls. Pull off the side of the road so as not to block traffic.

Winter

Spring

Dusk

Tina Karle

Chain Mill Falls

Rating 3

The steps of a good man are ordered by the Lord, And He delights in his way. Psalm 37:23

Height: 10/40 Feet	Restrooms: No
Water: Spring/ Winter	Access: Easy
Form: Drop	Distance: Roadside
Coordinates: 38.41.67 N 85.28.31 W	Bench: No

Trail
From the roadside, walk into the woods for a short way to view the falls. Use caution as there is no guardrail and there are small steep cliffs; and the hillside can be slippery. The larger set of Chain Mill Falls can only be seen in the winter from the location of Fremont Falls.

Directions
In Hanover, across from the Spring Hill Golf Course take a left onto Tull Road. Pass Butler Falls and continue down the road. Before you come to the T in the road, pull off on your right and cross the road to see the set of falls. The larger set of falls is located on private property.

Main Falls

Postcard

Clifty Falls

Rating 4

Clifty Falls was established as a state park in 1920. In 1965 almost 700 acres of fields and woods were added to the park as recreational areas. Due to winters thaw and spring rains the falls are best viewed from November through June. July through October the falls are usually at a lower if any rate of flow. There are scenic bluff top views of the Ohio River and the Madison area. Towering above the tree's Clifty Creek Power Plant smoke stacks can be seen as well. There are many tributary creeks throughout the park that has waterfalls not listed in the trail brochure. Picnicking can be had at several shelters in the park. Class A camping is also available. Lunch is available as well as overnight stays at the Clifty Inn. During summer months there is a fee. April through October the Park charges a fee based on if you are from Indiana or out of state.

Height: 10/15/20/30/50/70/80 Feet	Restrooms: Summer Months Only
Water: Spring/Winter	Access: Moderate to Hard
Form: Drop/Cascade	Distance: Roadside to 2 Miles
Coordinates: 38.45.25 N 85.25.21 W 38.45.47 N 85.25.82 W Tunnel 38.46.16 N 85.26.04 W Little Clifty	Bench: Yes Fee: Yes

Trail

Pick up a trail map at either end of the park. This hike will start from down at Route 56, coming north into the park. After driving into the park, pull off after you have crossed the large creek bridge. Walk back onto the bridge and look to your left for a view of Little Crooked Creek's waterfall. In the winter off to the right is another large falls you can see through the trees. Continue driving north through the park, passing a small cascade to your right as you are driving. The next waterfall will be at Hoffman Falls. Take the sometimes slippery when wet wooden steps down to the overlook to gain a view of the falls. After leaving Hoffman Falls, pull over at the small pull-off to see another small set of falls that's on the main branch for Hoffman. After a good rain there is another side falls coming in next to the main falls. Continue on your drive and stop at the Lilly Memorial Parking Lot. Walk to your right and head down the many sets of steps. Once down on the trail look to your right at the cascading waterfall that are next to the steps. Look over the walking bridge to your left to see another 10-foot falls, which empty into Clifty Creek. You are now on trail 4. You can make your way down to trail 2 which pretty much walks up Clifty Creek or you can stay on trail 4 which will take you to trail 5, which goes past an old railroad tunnel. If you brought a flashlight with you, you can explore the tunnel, which does go all the way through. As of this writing I believe they may have closed the tunnel to further exploration. Retrace your steps or form a loop via the park road back to Lilly Memorial. Continue driving north and stop at Tunnel Falls. Steps lead you down to an overlook. Walk past the overlook walking to your left on trail 5. After a good rain there is another waterfall that goes over the trail and on over the cliff. Great photo shots can be had of the side falls and Tunnel Falls in the background. There are different views of Tunnel Falls to be had as you walk back toward the overlook to Tunnel Falls.. Climb back up the steps and continue your drive north stopping at the next pull off. Walk over to the stonewall and look across the valley to see an over view of Big Clifty Falls. There is also another side waterfall here as well next to the overview. It is a seasonal falls. Continue on your drive north turning left to go into the parking lot area for Big and Little Clifty Falls. Walk toward the shelter house and on past, down a rocky area to view Big Clifty Falls up close. Take the trail to your left, which will lead you down some wooden steps and to your left you will come to an overlook and more wooden steps leading down to a creek bridge. From here you can see a side view of Little Clifty. Down on the bridge you can get a giddy feeling as the water is rushing underneath you and on over the drop of Little Clifty. Look upstream for other smaller falls as well. Continue on up the steps stopping to see another view of Little Clifty. Continue on down the trail coming to a side falls that's right by the trail bridge. Up further is another set of falls on the main stream. Retrace your steps back

Tina Karle

to the parking lot from here. Consulting the trail map can have longer hikes and deciding how far of a walk you wish to take while here in the park.

Directions

From the town of Madison, go west on Route 56 and the park will be on your right hand side.

Little Crooked Creek Falls Winter

Summer

Fall

Spring

Side falls upstream from Hoffman Falls

Side Falls

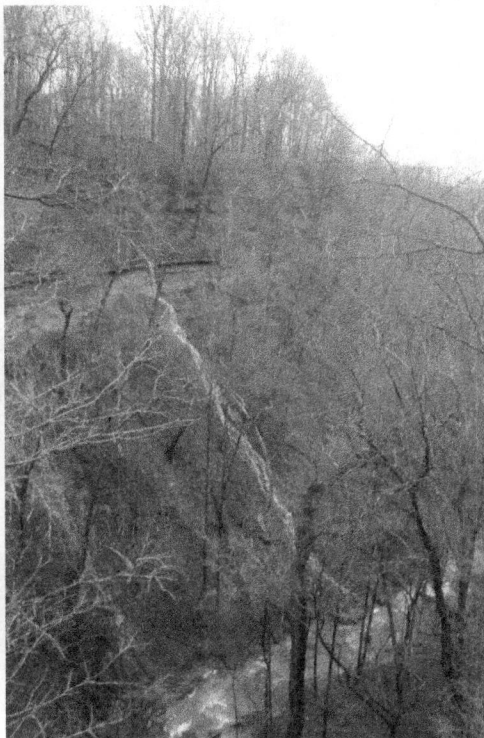

After heavy rain intermittent falls

Tina Karle

Hoffman Falls

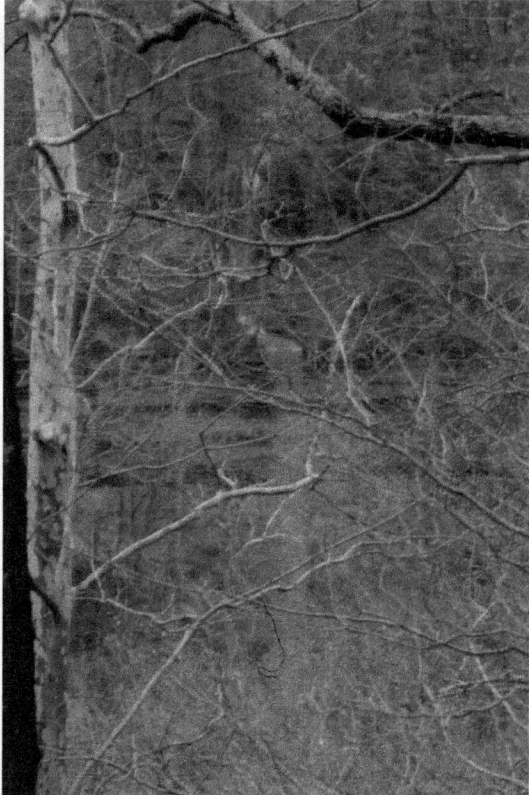

Wallace Falls

Lilly Memorial Pull-Off area

falls below the bridge

Lilly Memorial upper and lower falls

Tunnel Falls

Side falls up from Tunnel Falls

Tina Karle

Side Stream

Little Clifty Falls

Big Clifty late winter

Fall

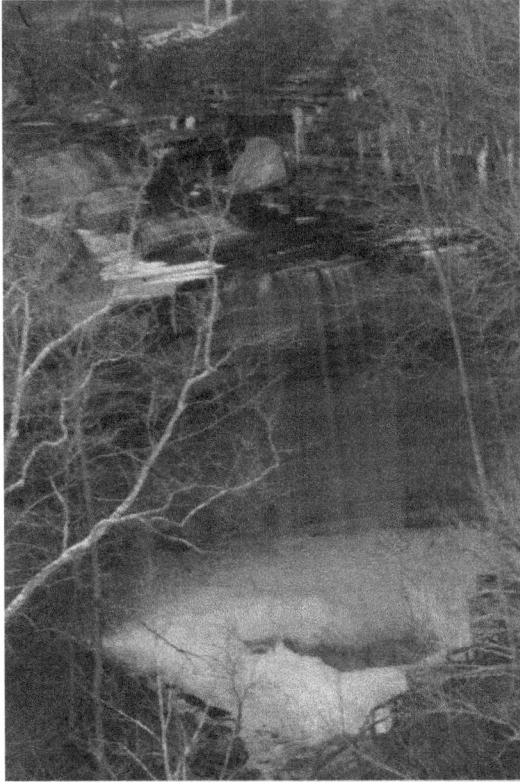

Big Clifty Winter

Tunnel Falls Winter

Upstream of Little Clifty

Tina Karle

Side View of Little Clifty

Little Clifty

Bridge over Little Clifty

Crooked Creek Falls

Rating 3

And I will make My mountains into level paths for them; the highways shall be raised above the valleys.
Isaiah 49:11

Height:4 Feet	Restrooms: No
Water: Spring/Winter	Access: Moderate
Form: Cascade	Distance: Roadside
Coordinates: 38.46.50 N 85.21.84 W	Bench: No

Trail
From the edge of the road, carefully make your way down the small incline to the creeks edge. From here you can view the beautiful cascading set of falls. Respect homeowner's property and visit the falls only.

Directions
In downtown Madison take Route 421 going north for 2.5 miles. Make a U turn at Old State Route 62. Take the first right onto Old State Route 62 and turn right. Proceed until the end of the road. Do NOT drive onto the private property. The falls will be on your right and there is a small place to turn around.

Tina Karle

Crosley Lake Falls

Rating 4

Crosley Lake is a reservoir located just 3.9 miles from North Vernon, in the state of Indiana, United States. Fishermen will find a variety of fish including brown trout, bluegill and northern pike here. So grab your favorite fly fishing rod and reel, and head out to Crosley Lake. Crosley Lake is on a tributary of Vernon Fork River in Jennings County, Indiana and is used for recreation purposes. It has been been there since 1937. It has a normal surface area of 15.1 acres. It is owned by Indiana Department of Natural Resources. Crosley Lake Dam is of earthen construction. Its height is 27 feet with a length of 290 feet. Maximum discharge is 864 cubic feet per second. Its capacity is 204 acre feet. Normal storage is 136 acre feet. It drains an area of 0.94 square miles.

Height: 10 Feet	Restrooms: No
Water: Spring/Winter	Access: Moderate
Form: Cascade	Distance: 1000 Feet
Coordinates: 38.57.38 N 85.35.52 W	Bench: No

Trail

From the gravel parking area, walk across the earthen dam to the water spillway. You will need wet shoes to cross this driveway area. Once across, head into the woods towards your left, heading downhill along the faint path, which will lead you over to the edge of the slope. From here you can gain a perfect view of the cascading falls! Use caution as the rocks down in the creek can be quite slippery! Return the way you came.

Directions

From downtown North Vernon head south on Route 3. Turn left into the Crosley Lake Ranger area and information. Drive behind the building, taking the gravel road back through the woods to the dead end parking area.

From the edge view

base of the falls view

46

Looking down on the falls

top of the falls

Crosley Lake

Overspill Road

Tina Karle

Deadmans Falls

Rating 3

But when the hot weather arrives, the water disappears. The brook vanishes in the heat. Job 6:17

Height: 6 Feet	Restrooms: No
Water: Spring/Winter	Access: Moderate
Form: Tiered/Drop	Distance: 700 Feet
Coordinates: 38.43.39 N 85.27.55 W	Bench: No

Trail
From edge of the road, make your way down to the creek through the woods. There isn't a trail, just the one that you make for yourself. The first waterfall is near the gated driveway. To see the falls from the creek, walk past the falls and around the rock ledge and use the trees for a guide down to the creek. To see the other set of falls, back up in the woods, go back to the road and walk down to where the guardrail starts. Pick your way down the small steep hill and walk over to the small cliff edge. Looking to your left up the creek you will see both sets of falls. Walk back the way you came.

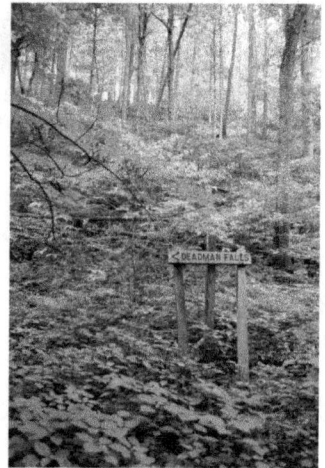

Directions
From Route 62 in Hanover, turn into the Hanover College Entrance, the roads name is Lucina Ball Drive. Follow the road till you come to the driveway on your left with the locked gated fence. Pull off to the side taking care not to block the driveway and walk into the woods to your right to see the falls.

Winter side view

Base view of lower falls

Halfway up hillside view

48

Fall at Dead Man's Falls

Author and husband spring at upper falls

Winter at Dead Man's Falls

Spring cliff edge view

View of middle and upper falls

Deer Path Falls

Rating 3

A white tailed deer drinks from the creek; I want to drink God, deep draughts of God. Psalms 42:1

Height: 5/10 Feet	Restrooms: No
Water: Spring/Winter	Access: Moderate
Form: Drop/Cascade	Distance: Roadside
Coordinates: 38.51.83 N 85.19.54 W	Bench: No

Trail

If you wish to see these falls closer than a roadside view, make your way down the small slope; cross the tiny stream, and climb up to the other bank, and make your way through the sticker bushes to see this set of falls. A small traverse up a slope will reveal another view of the five foot cascade upstream.

a

Directions

From the tiny town of Rexville, on Route 421 turn east onto Route 250. Take a left when the road ends onto N Graham Road. Turn right at .16th of a mile onto Route 250. Follow along the curvy road for about three and half miles. The falls will be to your right about the half mile mark on the speedometer. There will be a guardrail you need to park up from.

Dry Falls

Rating 2

Though in the morning it springs up new, by evening it is dry and withered. Psalms 90:6

Height: 25 Feet	Restrooms: No
Water: Spring/Winter	Access: Easy
Form: Tier	Distance: Roadside
Coordinates: 38.46.71 N 85.21.36 W	Bench: No

Trail
From the edge of the road, walk over to the guardrail to view this road side falls! This falls runs only after a good rain!

Directions
From downtown Madison, turn and drive north on Route 421. After you pass the road for Old Route 62 the falls will come up on your right within less than .2 miles.

Tina Karle

Dry Fork Creek

Rating 2

For He orders His angels to protect you wherever you go. They will steady you with their hands to keep you from stumbling against the rocks on the trail. Psalms 91:11,12

Height: 4 Feet	Restrooms: No
Water: Spring/Winter	Access: Moderate
Form: Cascade	Distance: 500 Feet
Coordinates: 38.50.11 N 85.18.25 W	Bench: No

Trail

Carefully make your way from the edge of the road, down the slope to the creeks edge. Rock hop your way across the creek to the junction of the second creek. Carefully make your way crossing the rocks to the side of the second creek. Walk upstream to the falls. During heavy rain, the current is quite strong and caution must be observed as the rocks are unsteady and slippery.

Directions

From downtown Madison Indiana turn left onto Route 421 and travel 3.3 miles. Turn right onto Route 62 and drive 3.8 miles. Continue onto N China/Manville Road. Turn left at County Road 525/ E Lower Dry Fork Road and drive 1.7 miles. Turn left at N Whippoorwill Road and travel less than .1 miles. The falls are on the right hand side of the road. If you cross the creek that goes across the road you have gone too far.

Dugan Hollow Road Falls

Rating 3

The water leaps and rushes over the rocks. Flying through the air it sparkles; each drop a jewel in a moving symphony. The water rumbles and mumbles moves and grooves, yet still remains the same. Water hitting the rock with a noticeable splash as it returns once more to join the other many drops which gather for a moment in the pool below before heading more slowly this time down the creek in its quieter journey, the drops mingled now as one drifts away, as the waterfall thunders on.

Height: 15 Feet	Restrooms: No
Water: Spring/Winter	Access: Moderate to easy
Form: Tier	Distance: Roadside
Coordinates: 38.45.08 N 85.21.66 W	Bench: No

Trail
From the edge of the pull off, walk over to the edge of the slope to view this cascading set of falls. This falls runs best after a hard rain.

Directions
From downtown Madison turn and go north on Route 421 for less than a mile. Turn right onto Aulenbach Road. Continue driving up the hill. The road changes name to Dugan Hollow Road. Drive .8 miles to the pull off located on the left hand side of the road at the bend. Falls are to your left.

Eagle Hollow Falls

Rating 2

They were forced to live in the dry stream beds, among the rocks and in holes in the ground. Job 30:6

Height: 5 Feet		Restrooms: No	
Water: Spring/Winter		Access: Moderate	
Form: Cascade		Distance: 200 Feet	
Coordinates: 38.45.16 N 85.20.03 W		Bench: No	

Trail
From the edge of the road make your way into the stream bed and walk up the rock strewn creek to the base of the falls. Use caution after a heavy rain!

Directions
From downtown Madison head east on Route 56 for 2.2 Miles. Turn left onto Eagle Hollow Road and drive about .9 miles to the small pull off located on the right hand side of the road.

Farmers Retreat Falls

Rating 2

He casts forth His ice as fragments; who can stand before His cold? Job 38:30

Height: 4/5 Feet	Restrooms: No
Water: Spring/Winter	Access: Easy
Form: Cascade	Distance: Roadside
Coordinates: 38.58.99 N 85.05.31 W 38.58.97 N 85.05.14 W	Bench: No

Trail

From the edge of the road, carefully make your way down to the creek. Rock hop your way upstream to the juncture of both streams. From here you can go either way to view unique sets of falls! Use caution after a heavy rain, the rocks are unstable and quite slippery!

Directions

In Madison turn north onto Route 421 and drive 16.6 miles. Turn right onto W County Road 800s and drive 6.7 miles. W County road 800S becomes Route 62. Turn right to stay on Route 62. Turn right to stay on Route 62/Friendship Road and drive another 4.1 miles. The falls will be located on your right with a small pull off.

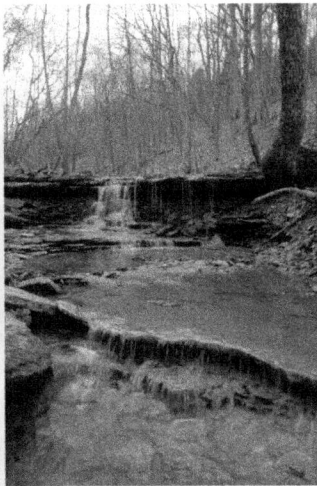

Right side of stream   left side stream   Main stream upper

View of both falls   winter view of both falls

Right side of creek winter

Left branch creek

Close up of right main falls

Right side of falls spring

view of both sets of falls spring

Rating 4

And I heard a voice from heaven like the sound of great waters and like the rumbling of mighty thunder: the voice I heard (seemed like the music) of harpists accompanying themselves on their harps. Rev 14:2

Height: 35 Feet	Restrooms: No
Water: Spring/Winter	Access: Easy
Form: Cascade/drop	Distance: Roadside
Coordinates: 38.45.07 N 85.23.66W	Bench: No

Trail
From your car walk around the small area to view the falls from all angles, even from behind the falling water! You can even drive behind the falls when you go to leave!

Directions
From Route 56 in Madison, turn north onto Route 7. The falls will be on your right partially up the hill at a bend in the road.

Hanover Beach Hill Falls

Rating 2

When the poor and needy seek water, and there is none, and their tongue faileth for thirst, I the Lord will hear them, I the God of Israel will not forsake them. Isaiah 41:17

Height: 50 Feet	Restrooms: No
Water: Spring/Winter	Access: Easy/Hard
Form: Tiered	Distance: ¼ Mile to bottom
Coordinates: 38.42.76 N 85.27.94 W	Bench: No

Trail
Take the faint trail on the left side of the road, which angles down by the cliff edge. Side views can be seen of this falls from the trail. If you want to see the full view of these falls you must go off the trail and pick your way down the semi steep hill. Make your way over to the bottom of the falls. Return the way you came. For a much longer hike, cross over the waste pipe and take the trail, which leads over to Crowe Falls for an extended hike in this area.

Directions
From Route 56 going southwest, turn left onto Main Street/Ball Drive. Turn right onto Hanover Beach Hill Road and drive about 300-feet to the pull-off on the right. The trail starts near the road.

Winter view of the falls

Side falls downstream

Spring view of the falls

Tina Karle

Hatcher Hill Falls

Rating 3

His branches shall spread; His beauty shall be like an olive tree, And His fragrance like Lebanon. Hosea 14:6

Height: 5/15 Feet	Restrooms: No
Water: Spring/Winter	Access: Easy
Form: Cascade	Distance: ¼ Mile
Coordinates: 38.45.56 N 85.22.10 W	Bench: No

Trail
From the guardrail walk past the post with the blinky red light to the creek to view the first five-foot waterfall. Walk around the guardrail to the abandoned road, and walk down the road, watching to your right for views of many falls. Return the way you came.

Directions
From Route 7 at the fork in Madison, take Green Road. Drive across the street at the stop sign. Bear to the right at Hatcher Hill Road and go to the dead-end street that has a guardrail blocking the road. Park off to the side of the road.

Huckleberry Branch Falls

Rating 3

For He caused gushing streams to burst from flinty rock. Psalms 114:8

Height: 3 Feet	Restrooms: No
Water: Year	Access: Easy
Form: Tier	Distance: Roadside
Coordinates: 39.00.49 N 85.33.14 W	Bench: No

Trail
From the edge of the road, walk into the brush to the creeks edge to see this tiered set of falls.

Directions
In North Vernon take Route 50 heading east for 4.1 miles. Take a sharp right onto N County Road 280 E and drive .7 miles. Turn left at E County Road 200 N and drive a half mile. Take the first right onto N County Road 325 E and drive .4 miles to the falls located on your right.

Indian Kentuck Cemetery

Rating 2

He split open the rocks in the wilderness to give them plenty of water, as though gushing from a spring!
Psalm 78:16

Height: 5 Feet	Restrooms: No
Water: Spring/Winter	Access: Moderate
Form: Tier	Distance: 500 Feet
Coordinates: 38.52.32 N 85.19.35 W	Bench: No

Trail
From the back of the cemetery enter the woods and pick your way down the hill to the creek. There is no set trail here accept for the one that you make. Once down to the creeks edge rock hop across the first stream to the small island. From here you can gain views of both sets of falls. During low water hunt for the small spring found at the base of the falls. Return the way you came.

Directions
From downtown Madison turn left onto Route 421 and travel 6.9 miles. Turn right at IN-250 and drive .6 miles. Turn left at IN-250/N Graham Road. Take the first right onto IN 250 E and travel 1.7 miles. Turn left at N Copeland Ridge Road and drive .8 miles to the cemetery located on your right. Pull off the road so as not to block traffic. Watch for the concrete blocks in the ditch.

Second set late winter   First set of falls winter   Early spring

Indian Kentuck Cemetery

Both sets of falls after a heavy spring rain

Little Bull Creek Falls

Rating 4

You started the springs and rivers, sent them flowing among the hills. All the wild animals now drink their fill, Psalms 104:10

Height: 10/15/20 Feet	Restrooms: No
Water: Spring/Winter	Access: Easy
Form: Cascade/Tiered	Distance: Roadside
Coordinates: 38.29.19 N 85.31.88 W	Bench: No

Trail
There are five waterfalls here for you to enjoy! Some are running better than others, but worth the little jaunt to see them! The first falls is roadside back a few feet across from the low road bridge. The main falls are in the creek and good wet shoes are required, as the rocks are extremely slippery. The third falls are downstream and they come into the main creek from the left side. A very slippery but carefully placed footing will bring you downstream a slight ways gives you a view of these side falls. On your right side of the creek is a small faint falls that cascades into the creek as well. If you wish, you can drive further up the hill toward the top and on your right is the last of the falls. It is a tiered drop and it slides downstream to cascade into the main Little Bull Creek. Respect people's privacy and don't block the driveways!

Directions
From Charlestown, go north on Route 62. Turn right onto Vesta Road, follow until you come to Charlestown Bethlehem Road. Turn left onto Charlestown Bethlehem Road. Turn right onto Graebe Road, and the falls are right where you cross the really low road bridge.

Old Road bridge

New Road Bridge

Roadside Falls

Side falls further down stream

Further up the road at the dead end last set of falls

London Road Falls

Rating 2

You will surely forget your trouble, recalling it only a waters gone by. Job 11:16

Height: 50 Feet	Restrooms: No
Water: Spring/Winter	Access: Moderate
Form: Slide	Distance: 500 Feet
Coordinates: 38.38.94 N 85.27.26 W	Bench: No

Trail
Walk down the road a few feet to find an easy access over the slight hill that's towards your left. Walk down the other side of the hill to the stream. Use caution seeing these falls, as the rocks in the stream are quite slippery. The falls resemble a huge waterslide but I believe isn't safe to do so; but is unique all the same!

Directions
From Hanover, go south on Route 62 and turn left onto W New Bethel Road. The road changes names and becomes W Prospect Road. Follow the road and turn a hard right at the bend and then a left still staying on W Prospect Road. Pass a small road to your left and the falls will be by a slight pull off in the road on the right hand side.

Tina Karle

Lost Fork Road Falls

Rating 3

They'll be like dew from God, like summer showers not mentioned in the weather forecast, not subject to calculation or control. Micah 5:7

Height: 4 Feet	Restrooms: No
Water: Spring/Winter	Access: Moderate
Form: Cascade	Distance: Roadside
Coordinates: 38.43.84 N 85.10.37 W	Bench: No

Trail
From the edge of the road, make your way down the slope to the creeks edge. Rock hop over to the downed tree to view this unusual set of falls.

Directions
From downtown Madison head east on Route 56 for about 8.2 miles. Turn left onto Lost Fork Road and drive 3.5 miles to a small area where there is a gated drive. Pull over by the gate and walk across the road to view the falls.

Spring

Early Spring

Lowery Lane Falls

Rating 2

Let my teaching fall like rain, and my words descend like dew, like showers on new grass, like abundant rain on tender plants. Deuteronomy 32:2

Height: 5 Feet	Restrooms: No
Water: Spring/Winter	Access: Easy
Form: Drop	Distance: Roadside
Coordinates: 38.42.73 N 85.28.10 W	Bench: No

Trail
A quick hop from your car brings you to the edge of the road and a walk over to the cliff edge to peer towards your left to see this set of falls.

Directions
From Main Street in downtown Madison stay on Route 56. Take the slight right to stay on Route 56 and drive 4.7 miles. Turn left at N Main Cross Street. Take the second left onto Locust Street. Turn left at 1st Street. Turn right at Pine Ridge Road. Take the first left onto Lowery Lane and drive less than .1 miles and pull over to the edge of the road.

Winter view   Spring view

Tina Karle

Lucina Ball Drive Falls

Rating 4

In all your ways acknowledge Him, and He will make your paths straight. Proverbs 3:6

Height: 11 Feet	Restrooms: No
Water: Spring/Winter	Access: Moderate
From: Drop	Distance: 800 Feet
Coordinates: 38.43.30 N 85.27.68 W	Bench: No

Trail
From the edge of the road to your right, walk into the woods, following the creek on the faint trail. Walk down into the creek and rock hop to the edge of the pool to see the waterfall. There is a nice rock overhang that expands the sound of the falls. Return the way you came.

Directions
From Route 56 near Hanover turn into the Hanover College Entrance. This is Lucina Ball Drive. Pass Deadmans Falls; and the bend you make to your left pull over in front of the guardrail. To your right, past the guardrail is the faint path. Also, across the street over the guardrail is Scenic Drive Falls.

70

Michigan Road Falls

Rating 2

It dwells on a cliff and stays there at night; a rocky crag is its stronghold. Job 39:28

Height: 15 Feet	Restrooms: No
Water: Spring/Winter	Access: Easy
Form: Drop	Distance: Roadside
Coordinates: 38.44.74 N 85.23.22 W	Bench: No

Trail
From the edge of the road walk over the cliff face to view this intermittent set of falls.

Directions
From downtown Madison on Route 56 turn left onto Michigan Road. Drive north about .4 miles to the rock cliff located on the right hand side. Pull off onto the verge of the road so as not to block traffic to see this set of falls.

Tina Karle

Muscatatuck County Park

Rating 3

This park was first known as Vinegar Mills Park. In the 1830's Vinegar Mill operated as a water powered mill on the Muscatatuck River. Muscatatuck is a Delaware Indian word which means, Clear River or land of the winding waters. There is a double spring located in the park that cascades down a rocky slope into the intermittent ravine creek. Scenic waterfalls abound through out the park.

Height: 3/10 Feet	Restrooms: No
Water: Spring/Winter	Access: Moderate
Form: Cascade	Distance: ¼ Mile
Coordinates: 38.59.37 N 85.37.14 W	Bench: No

Vinegar Mill Trail:
From the parking lot, go down the 57 stone steps and turn toward your right. Follow the trail up and over small mounds. The trail leads next to the intermittent stream. You may want to watch for small snakes as well sunbathing on the rocks during the summer. Within a few feet you come up to the double spring waterfall that runs almost year round; providing the water table is high enough. Continuing down the trail you come to another waterfall; where the trail stops. Return the way you came.

Shelter Trail:
From the shelter, walk over the bridge and go up to the road. Walk to your right down the road and look to your right down the ravine for views of Canyon River Falls. Also, you may take the trail around the wall and down next to the creek from the parking lot, for a closer view of these falls. To see yet another set of falls that are hidden within the park, walk back near the main road to the side creek on your right. Walk up the creek watching out for very large crawdads in the small stream; continue walking up the small stream to the tiny set of cascading falls. Return back the way you came.

Directions
In North Vernon on Route 7, go south to the park entrance, which is on your right. Stay to the left once entering the park and follow the windy road down ¼ mile to Vinegar Mill, which will be on your left. The shelter trail is another ¼ mile further down the road.

Canyon River Falls

Double Spring Waterfall

Small Falls on a side stream in the park

Tina Karle

Old State Route 62 Falls

Rating 2

We spring up like wildflowers in the desert and then wilt; transient as the shadow of a cloud. For a tree there is always hope. Chop it down and it still has a chance-its roots can put out fresh sprouts. Even if its roots are old and gnarled, its stump long dormant, at the first whiff of water it comes to life, buds and grows like a sapling. Like lakes and rivers that have dried up, parched reminders of what once was. Job 14:1

Height: 10 Feet	Restrooms: No
Water: Spring/Winter	Access: Easy
Form: Drop	Distance: Roadside
Coordinates: 38.46.61 N 85.21.30 W	Bench: Yes-Stone Wall

Trail
From the edge of the road walk over to the stone wall to view these falls. A closer look can be had by walking down the slope and picking your way up the stream.

Directions
From downtown Madison take Route 421 going north for 2.5 miles. Turn right onto Old State Route 62 and drive .3 miles to the pull off located on the left hand side of the road.

Olean Cemetery Falls

Rating 3

As heat and drought snatch away the melted snow, so the grave snatches away those who have sinned. Job 24:19

Height: 3 Feet	Restrooms: No
Water: Year	Access: Moderate
Form: Cascade	Distance: 1500 Feet
Coordinates: 38.59.33 N 85.13.28 W	Bench: No

Trail
Follow the old gravel road at the far right of the cemetery down to the creek. The falls are slightly downstream. Return the way you came.

Directions
From Versailles take Route 129 south for 5.8 miles to the turn off into Olean Cemetery located on your right.

Winter

Spring

Tina Karle

One Lane Road Falls

Rating 2

The Sovereign Lord is my strength; He makes my feet like the feet of a deer, He enables me to go on the heights. Habakkuk 3:19

Height: 3 Feet	Restrooms: No
Water: Spring/Winter	Access: Moderate
Form: Tier	Distance: Roadside
Coordinates: 38.55.76 N 85.07.82 W	Bench: No

Trail
From the edge of the road make your way over to the edge to view this cascading set of falls!

Directions
From Rising Sun take Route 56 going west for 1.9 miles. Turn right to stay on Route 56 and drive another 6.7 miles. Continue onto Aberdeen Road and drive 8.3 miles. Turn right at Bear Creek Road and drive about 1.9 miles to the falls located on your right.

Rating 3

But for good men the path is not uphill and rough! God does not give them a rough and treacherous path, but smoothes the road before them.

Height: 3 Feet	Restrooms: No
Water: Spring/Winter	Access: Moderate
Form: Cascade	Distance: Roadside
Coordinates: 38.58.45 N 85.36.24W	Bench: No

Trail

Make your way down the sloped hillside to view this tucked away set of falls along a busy road!

Directions

From Vernon Indiana drive south on Route 3/7. Where Route 3 and Route 7 splits go south on Route 3 for .4 miles to pull off along the verge of the road. The falls will be to your right if you are facing north.

Tina Karle

Route 7 Falls

Rating 3

Who is like unto thee, O Lord, among the gods? Who is like thee, glorious in holiness, fearful in praises, doing wonders? Exodus 15:11

Height: 25/30 Feet	Restrooms: No
Water: Spring/Winter	Access: Hard
Form: Cascade	Distance: Roadside to ½ mile
Coordinates: 38.45.08 N 85.23.77 W	Bench: No

Trail
From Hanging Rock Falls, cross the road using caution. Climb over the guardrail and walk up the road; going uphill, past the bend. In the early spring, late fall, and winter these two falls are easily seen from the road. If you wish to see them up close, make your way down to the old railroad tracks. It is best to walk up the road until you find an easy way onto the old tracks. Walk the tracks down hill, noting the side falls coming in next to the tracks and back to the small train bridge. Falls are right below you and next to you. Note the large falls across on the other hill by Route 7. Return back the way you came.

Directions
From Madison on Route 56, turn onto Route 7 going north, and park up the hill on your right next to Hanging Rock Falls.

Side falls by Rte 7   old railroad tracks

Roadside down below   along the railroad tracks

Falls located off edge of railroad tracks

Tina Karle

Route 56 Falls

Rating 4

If a Godly man compromises with the wicked, it is like polluting a fountain or muddying a spring. Proverbs 25:26

Height: 12 Feet	Restrooms: No
Water: Spring/Winter	Access: Moderate
Form: Cascade	Distance: 200 Feet
Coordinates: 38.44.24 N 85.26.69W	Bench: No

Trail

From the edge of the road, walk into the woods and make your way down the hill to the falls. For a rougher hike continue on down to the stream bed and follow the side stream up to another set of falls. Return the way you came.

Directions

Going southwest on Route 56, before you reach the top of the hill in Madison, there is a pullover on your left across from the fancy rock wall on your right. Park by the sign that says 40 mph that's in front of the guardrail. If there is a lot of trash over the small slope you are in the right area!

Winter

Spring

Rating 2

The Lord's love is eternal, it knows no boundaries. His love reaches us wherever we are, at any time, to make our hearts rejoice.

Height: 4 Feet	Restrooms: No
Water: Spring/Winter	Access: Easy
Form: Cascade	Distance: Roadside
Coordinates: 38.49.18 N 85.20.69 W	Bench: No

Trail
Pop out of your car and take a quick glance making sure there is not any cars coming! Take a quick picture and off you go!

Directions
Outside of China on Route 62, heading toward Madison, the falls will be on your right hand side.

Tina Karle

Route 421 Falls

Rating 3

Drive along the Northern road where you will encounter a watery abode. Step lightly from your car, and you won't go far to see a murmuring set of falls.

Height: 10 Feet	Restrooms: No
Water: Spring/Winter	Access: Easy
Form: Cascade	Distance: Roadside
Coordinates: 38.46.85 N 85.22.03 W	Bench: No

Trail
From the edge of the road, walk across the small grassy area to view the falls.

Directions
From Route 50, turn south onto Route 421 and go past Route 62; at the next road to your left, turn around and then take a right back onto Route 421 going north. Drive less than a fourth mile and park by the junction 62 sign. The falls are to your right.

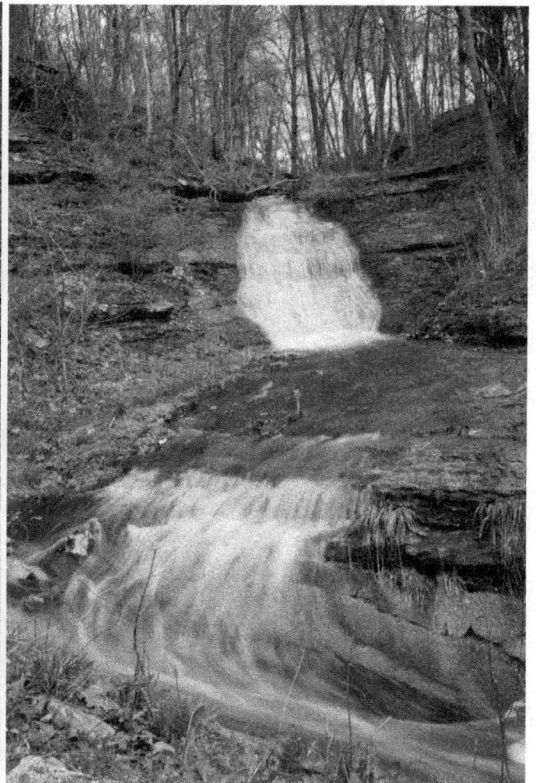

Winter   Spring

82

Rating 3

I will lead the blind by ways they have not known, along unfamiliar paths I will guide them; I will turn the darkness into light before them and make the rough places smooth. These are the things I will do; I will not forsake them. Isaiah 42:16

Height: 25 Feet	Restrooms: No
Water: Spring/Winter	Access: Hard
Form: Tiered	Distance: ¼ Mile
Coordinates: 38.43.30 N 85.27.60 W	Bench: No

Trail
This is a tough hike. You have to make your own trail to get down to the base of the falls. Cross over the guardrail and pick your best way down the steep hill to the bottom of the falls. In the spring this hike is worth the effort as the falls are beautiful to see. Make your way back the way you came.

Directions
From Route 56 near Hanover, turn into the Hanover College Entrance. This is Lucina Ball Drive. Pass Deadmans Falls and at the bend you make to your left, pull over in front of the guardrail. Cross the road to the falls. Note: Lucina Ball Falls are to your right.

Tina Karle

Signor Hill Road Falls

Rating 3

He waters the furrows with abundant rain. Showers soften the earth, melting the clods and causing seeds to sprout across the land. Psalms 65:12

Height: 3/4/8 Feet	Restrooms: No
Water: Spring/Winter	Access: Moderate
Form: Cascade/Drop	Distance: 1000 Feet
Coordinates: 39.00.28 N 85.13.78 W 39.00.26 N 85.13.72 W	Bench: No

Trail
Make your way down the hill and into the woods. Pick your way towards the creek and the first set of falls. Use caution in the pool around this falls as the mud is very soft and you will sink down quickly. From here rock hopping is a must to make your way downstream to see the other two sets of falls. After a rain there is a side falls on your right that is pretty to see. Use caution when making your way around the rocks as after a dry spell the rocks are very slippery. Return the way you came.

Directions
From Versailles take Route 50 going east to Route 421. Turn and go south on Route 421 for .4 miles. Turn left onto Route 129 and travel 4.5 miles to Signor Hill Road. Turn left onto Signor Hill Road and pull off there at the corner.

First Set of falls

Middle set of falls

Last set of falls

84

Sunrise Golf Course

Rating 4

This is an 18-hole golf course. The back 9 holes are from the original course and the front 9 were established by the city in the 1970's. Tee times are taken on the weekend and on holidays. There is also a fully stocked pro shop, snack bar that serves hot food, putting green, and two lovely waterfalls located in a ravine on the backside of the course.

Height: 10/12/40 Feet	Restrooms: Yes
Water: Spring/Winter	Access: Moderate to Hard
Form: Cascade	Distance: ½ Mile one way
Coordinates: bridge: 38.45.98 N 85.23.30W Big falls 38.45.95 N 85.22.95 W	Bench: No

Trail
Take the golf cart trail past the snack bar and walk the golf cart trail that takes you along the small creek. When you come to the bridge, go to your left and pick your way down past the small rock face to the creek. Two waterfalls are located under and beside the bridge. From here rock hop your way down the creek away from the bridge till you come to the top of the last waterfall. Take the faint trail on your left to the side and make your way down the steep hill to the base of the falls. Return back the way you came. Use caution during or after a hard rain as the hillside is quite slippery.

Directions
From Madison on Route 62 (E Clifty Drive) go south on Michigan Road. The Golf Course is about a half mile down the road on your left.

Tina Karle

Both sets of side falls by the bridge

Tina Karle

Sweet Water Road Falls

Rating 2

So Moses cried out in prayer to God. God pointed him to a stick of wood. Moses threw it into the water and the water turned sweet. Exodus 15:25

Height: 5 Feet	Restrooms: No
Water: Spring/Winter	Access: Moderate
Form: Cascade	Distance: Roadside
Coordinates: 38.49.14 N 85.16.46 W	Bench: No

Trail
From the edge of the road carefully make your way down to the stream by the old rock wall. Enjoy views of the falls creek side before climbing your way back up to the road.

Directions
In Madison turn left onto Route 421. Drive 3.3 miles. Turn right at Route 62 and drive 3.8 miles. Continue onto N China/Mainville Road and drive 2.6 miles. Turn left at N Turkey Branch Road and drive 1.8 miles. Continue straight onto County Road 566 for a half mile. Turn right onto N Sweet Water Road and drive about .8 miles to the falls which will be located on your right.

Late winter

Fall

Thornton Road Falls

Rating 4

You have made a wide path for my feet to keep them from slipping. Psalms 8:36

Height: 6/8/15 Feet	Restrooms: No
Water: Spring/Winter	Access: Moderate
Form: Cascade	Distance: Roadside to ¼ Mile
Coordinates: 38.53.03 N 85.20.14 W 38.52.81 N 85.20.13 W	Bench: No

Trail

From the edge of the road, carefully make your way down the slope near the road bridge heading upstream. Use your best judgment at finding the right path to get to the upper falls. Use caution around this upper set of falls as the rocks are very slippery. The creek above the upper falls is quite slippery even in lower water flow. Caution is advised if you wish to cross the creek above the falls. After viewing this set of falls carefully make your way back to the road. Walk up the road towards the hill and look for a faint atv trail on your left. Enter into the woods and follow this faint trail passing over a side falls along the way. Shortly you will see the slope that takes you down towards the creek and the last set of falls. Use caution as you make your way down the slope to the creek to view this set of falls. During high water it is not advised to get near the creek as the current is extremely strong. Return the way you came.

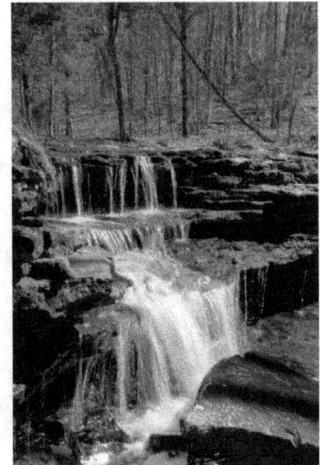

Directions

From downtown Madison turn left onto Route 421 and travel 9.9 miles. Turn right at E Thornton Road and drive 1.1 miles. Turn left to stay on E Thornton Road. Take the first right to stay on E Thornton Road. Continue onto County Road 200 E. Turn right at E Thornton Road and drive until you come to the main creek bridge. Find a spot to pull over where you are not blocking traffic.

View from the bridge

Closer view

Tina Karle

Spring upper set

Lower Main Falls

Side Falls along the way to lower Main Falls

Main Falls

upper falls by bridge

Tull Road Falls

Rating 2

I will praise the Lord according to His righteousness, and will sing praise to the name of the Lord most High. Psalm 7:17

Height: 20 Feet	Restrooms: No
Water: Spring/Winter	Access: Moderate
Form: Tiered	Distance: 500 Feet
Coordinates: 38.42.19 N 85.28.50 W	Bench: No

Trail

Walk up the road to where the creek crosses under the road; or if you have come to see Butler Falls make your way down to the creek and walk along the creek to where the falls comes in from the side. This falls is best viewed across the main creek. You can continue your hike on to see Butler falls, which is less than a couple of yards down the stream. Use caution, as there are no paths by the creek and the terrain is quite rough. Return the way you came heading back upstream.

Directions

From Route 56 in Hanover, turn left onto N Main Cross Street. Continue straight and turn left onto Tull Road. A golf course is across the street on your right as a land marker. Pull-off to the side of the road being sure not to block traffic.

Winter base view

Across the stream view

spring

Tina Karle

Vulture Falls

Rating 2

Perfectly at home on the high cliff face, invulnerable on pinnacle and crag? From her perch she searches for prey, spies it at a great distance. Her young gorge themselves on carrion; wherever there's a road kill, you'll see her circling. Job 39:26

Height: 10 Feet	Restrooms: No
Water: Spring/Winter	Access: Easy
Form: Cascade	Distance: Roadside
Coordinates: 38.45.09 N 85.21.56 W	Bench: Yes-Wall

Trail

From the edge of the road, walk over to the wall to view this set of falls. Vultures are usually around this area due to people throwing refuse down by the catch basin.

Directions

From downtown Madison turn left onto Route 421 and drive .6 miles. Turn right onto Aulenbach Ave. Continue on Aulenbach Ave, which changes names and becomes Dugan Hollow Road. Drive .7 miles to the pull off located on the left hand side of the road.

White Road Falls

Rating 4

The waterfall creates wind full of mist as it blows on my face, sparkling and glittering it flows through the air ever so light as it then floats to the ground. Reaching out for it I feel the wet little drops trailing down which draws my attention looking down at the bubbly white foam trailing down an away; water flowing like music to the ears.

Height: 3 ½ Feet	Restrooms: No
Water: Spring/Winter	Access: Easy
Form: Cascade	Distance: Roadside
Coordinates: 38.55.82 N 84.56.98 W	Bench: No

Trail
From the edge of the road, walk to the middle of the creek bridge and look down to see this cascading falls. To reach the bottom a tiny bit of climbing is necessary down a slippery rock and mud section next to the bridge to reach the edge of the creek. During the winter this section is muddy and slick so use caution.

Directions
In Dillsboro, take Route 262 and head south for 3.3 miles. Turn right to stay on Route 262 and drive another 4.1 miles. Turn right at Cass-Union Road and drive 1.7 miles. Turn left at White Road and drive about 1.7 miles to the creek bridge. Pull off alongside the edge of the road to see the falls.

Late fall

Spring

Side view

bridge view

Barking Dog Falls

Rating 4

Drops and drops of rain descending with thousand an millions joining till a mighty torrent flowing, gives in to gravity descending. Cascading liquid brightness, immense in power beauty to see, rainbows misting in the light reflecting beams for all our delight!

Height: 2/15 Feet	Restrooms: No
Water: Spring/Winter	Access: Moderate
Form: Drop	Distance: 1000 Feet
Coordinates: 38.52.58 N 85.21.71 W	Bench: No

Trail
From the edge of the road find the faint trail to the right of the creek. Follow the trail till it meanders to the creek and clamber and climb your way up the tree strewn creek to the base of the falls. Return the way you came.

Directions
Bryantsburg

Base of falls　　　　further downstream　　　　Roadside cascade

Tina Karle

Bascom Corner Falls

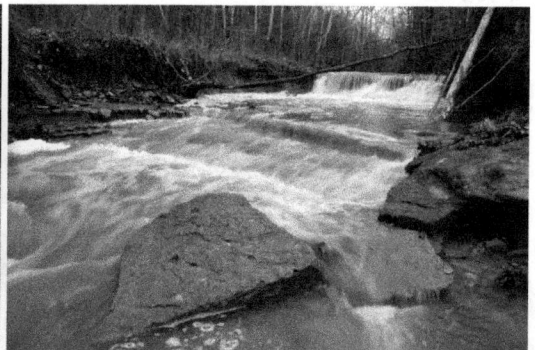

Rating 3

Around every bend, the river of God's goodness keeps our hearts in awe.

Height: 2/4 Feet	Restrooms: No
Water: Spring/Winter	Access: Moderate
Form: Cascade	Distance: 500 Yards
Coordinates: 38.55.77 N 84.57.01 W	Bench: No

Trail
Cross Arnold Creek and make your way up the side creek to this set of falls. Use caution during high water as the rocks are slippery and the water is deeper than it looks. Walking upstream along Arnold Creek, there is a one foot cascade where crossing is easier.

Directions
Bascom Corner

Different views of the falls

Bear Valley Road Falls

Rating 4

My mouth is filled with your praise declaring your splendor all day long. Psalms 71:8

Height: 5 Feet	Restrooms: No
Water: Year	Access: Easy
Form: Cascade	Distance: Roadside
Coordinates: 38.54.66 N 85.06.58 W	Bench: No

Trail
Walk over to the creek bridge and look upstream to gain a view of these beautiful set of falls. Do not trespass on the owner's property and enjoy the view of the falls only from the road bridge.

Directions
Aberdeen

Tina Karle

Rating 2

The voice of the Lord is upon the waters....Psalms 29:3

Height: 2 Feet	Restrooms: No
Water: Spring/Winter	Access: Moderate
Form: Cascade	Distance: 500 Feet
Coordinates: 38.58.05 N 85.36.17 W	Bench: No

From the edge of the road, make your way down the hillside to the creek. The falls are nestled by a small pool. Return up the hill the way you came.

Directions
Vernon

County Road 325 Falls

Rating 4

The sweet smell in the air lures you to the place where God shows His work. Water rumbling down the moisture soaked rocks and perfuming the air with the fresh moist smell of a spring waterfall.

Height: 5 Feet	Restrooms: No
Water: Spring/Winter	Access: Moderate
Form: Drop	Distance: 1000 Feet
Coordinates: 39.00.49 N 85.33.14 W	Bench: No

Trail
From the edge of the road by where the creek crosses the road, follow the faint path along the hillside keeping the main creek on your left. Walk up the side stream to the base of the falls. Return the way you have come.

Directions
North Vernon

Tina Karle

County Road 950 Falls

Rating 3

The sweet smell in the air lures you to the place where God shows His work. Water rumbling down the moisture soaked rocks and perfuming the air with the fresh moist smell of a spring waterfall.

Height: 7/20 Feet	Restrooms: No
Water: Spring/Winter	Access: Moderate to Hard
Form: Cascade/Drop	Distance: 200 Yards
Coordinates: 38.52.51 N 85.21.50 W	Bench: No

Trail
Make your way along the faint trail/old road to the first set of falls. During summer this falls is bone dry. The upper falls will actually look like a rocky wall. Cross where the creek flows and make your way onto the hillside. From here you can see the side view of the twenty foot falls when they are running.

Directions
Bryantsburg

Cragmont Street Falls

Rating 4

The waterfall creates wind full of mist as it blows on my face, sparkling and glittering it flows through the air ever so light as it floats to the ground. Reaching out for it I feel the wet little drops trailing down which draws my attention looking down at the bubbly white foam trailing down an away water flowing like music to the ears.

Height: 5/20 Feet	Restrooms: No
Water: Spring/Winter	Access: Moderate
Form: Drop/Cascade	Distance: 500 Feet
Coordinates: 38.44.98 N 85.23.62 W	Bench: No

Trail

From the edge of the road, walk over to see the first cascading set of falls by the large fallen rock. From here turn and start climbing up the hill on a diagonal and head towards the top of the creek above the first set of falls. Make your way down into the creek and carefully climb your way up the small falls and make your best way to the top and base of the top set of falls. Return back the way you came. Use caution descending as the rocks can be quite slippery.

Directions
Madison

Lower falls   Part way up   upper two falls

Tina Karle

Main Falls

Crooked Creek Main Falls

Rating 3

He gives me the surefootedness of a mountain goat upon the crags. He leads me safely along the top of the cliffs. Psalms 18:33

Height: 45 Feet	Restrooms: No
Water: Spring/Winter	Access: Hard
Form: Tiered	Distance: 1000 Feet
Coordinates: 38.46.93 N 85.22.17 W	Bench: No

Trail
Follow the GPS coordinates to find this unique set of falls!

Directions
Madison

 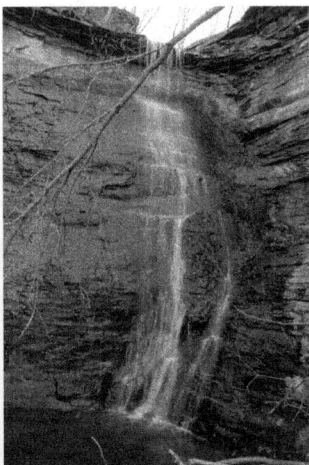 

Late winter   frontal view   frontal view

Side view

Tina Karle

Crowe Falls

Rating 4

Have I not commanded you? Be strong and of good courage; do not be afraid, nor be dismayed, for the Lord your God is with you wherever you go. Joshua 1:9

Height: 40 Feet	Restrooms: No
Water: Spring/Winter	Access: Moderate
Form: Cascade/Drop	Distance: ¼ Mile
Coordinates: 38.42.67N 85.27.85 W	Bench: No

Trail

Park by Hanover Beach Falls, and walk down the trail heading toward your left. Walk across the sanitation/waste pipe or rock hop across the creek. The trail heads to your left and then winds to the right following along the cliff edge. Continue walking ahead and the trail narrows as you are walking on a tiny rock outcrop ridge. Go down to your left using the tree roots for guidance. Look to your right at the lovely ten foot falls. Then walk or take a running jump across the stream, and take the path up and to your left. Stop at the small flat area and turn to see the side view of Crowe falls. Use caution here as the trail stays near the edge of the cliff. Return back the way you came going back over the stream. If you wish to see a frontal view of Crowe Falls, a hard hike is before you. You must pick your own way carefully down the hill near Hanover Beach Falls and cross the stream and find the side stream coming in to the main creek. Make your way up the rock strewn creek to the base of Crowe Falls. This isn't an easy hike especially come winter where the hillside is extremely slippery from snow fall!

Directions
Hanover

Side view of Crowe Falls

Ten Foot Cascade

Tip top of Crowe Falls

Tina Karle

Dobson Hollow Falls

Rating 3

Deep in the woods I hear an angels call. Tranquil and majestic a peaceful summer waterfall. Where the oaks and flowers shadow the stream, reflections play amid the dancing beams. I can smell the rain mixed with the juniper breeze washing my face clean. There ahead in the dancing mote laden path, a cascading jewel above a swirling pool. Upon the wind rides the angels call, tranquil and serene a quiet summer waterfall.

Height: 6/15 Feet	Restrooms: No
Water: Spring/Winter	Access: Moderate
Form: Cascade	Distance: ¼ Mile
Coordinates: 38.31.79 N 85.27.92 W	Bench: No

Trail

Do not let the dry creek fool you! Walk into the woods and follow the dry creek bed going into the woods. Follow along for a bit, crawling over and under a few downed trees. Continue to follow the creek until you come around a bend and you will see that there is water in the narrowed creek bed. Continue following upstream until you come to the first set of falls. Climb up the falls and continue upstream until you come to the larger final set of falls. Return the way you came. Will need bug spray if you visit during summer months as the mosquitoes are quite prevalent in the area!

Directions
New Washington

First set of falls

second set of falls

Third set of falls

Dugan Hollow Falls

Rating 3

They are like a man building a house, who dug down deep and laid the foundation on rock. When a flood came, the torrent struck that house but could not shake it, because it was well built.. Luke 6:48

Height: 10 Feet	Restrooms: No
Water: Spring/Winter	Access: Moderate
Form: Ramp/cascade	Distance: 200 Feet
Coordinates: 38.45.24 N 85.21.36 W	Bench: No

Trail
From the edge of the road, make your way down the slope to view this unique waterfall.

Directions
Madison

From on top of cliff   Base of falls

Tina Karle

E1033 Road Falls

Rating 2

An east wind from the Lord will come, blowing in from the desert; his spring will fail and his well dry up. Hosea 13:15

Height: 4/6 Feet	Restrooms: No
Water: Spring/Winter	Access: Moderate
Form: Cascade/Drop	Distance: 200 Feet
Coordinates: 38.53.16 N 85.22.29 W	Bench: No

Trail
From the edge of the road make your way down to the creeks edge. From here you can see the first cascading falls. Continue downstream to the last and larger set of falls. Note the side falls to your right as you are heading downstream. Return the way you came.

Directions
Bryantsburg

Side Falls

Main Falls

Upper first set of falls

Rating 3

And on every lofty mountain and every high hill there will be brooks running with water, Isaiah 30:25

Height: 108 Feet	Restrooms: No
Water: Spring/Winter	Access: Moderate
Form: Drop	Distance: 800 Feet
Coordinates: 38.41.63 N 85.28.15 W	Bench: No

Trail
From the edge of the road, walk across the small field and walk toward the large ravine. Pick your way down the slope picking your way over to the edge. Towards the left, there is a large tree trunk that is rotting near the edge, from here; you can gain your closest view of Freemont Falls. Another view would be to cross above Fremont and bushwhack through the woods until you gain a side view of this tall set of falls. This waterfall was measured with a surveyor's chain and my husbands help. So far for the record of falls we have measured for here in Indiana, Fremont tops off as the tallest free falling waterfall in the state that we have found so far.

Directions
Hanover

Winter view

spring view

Tina Karle

Harts Falls

Rating 4

I will make them and the places all around My hill a blessing; and I will cause showers to come down in their season; there shall be showers of blessing. Ezekiel 34:26

Height: 3/10/50 Feet	Restrooms: No
Water: Spring/Winter	Access: Moderate to Hard
Form: Cascade/Drop	Distance: ½ Mile one way
Coordinates: 38.40.62 N 85.27.50 W	Bench: No

Trail

Read this whole hike before attempting this hike. You shall get your feet wet on this hike! From the gravel area walk around the bend in the creek and you will come to the first set of falls. These falls are five feet in height; use caution climbing the small falls. Continue hiking up the creek until you encounter a large rocky area with a waterfall coming from between the two top most rocks and spilling into a small pool. To continue on to see the larger falls you can go one of two ways. To your left is a rocky scree that is easy to climb in the summer. It will put you up on top of the waterfall, which is to your right. The other way is to climb the hill part way, being observant as a resident bobcat makes his home in the lower hillside. Walk the hill following the creek past the ten-foot waterfall back down to the creek. Continue from on top of the waterfall going up the creek

and climbing fallen trees, clambering over rocks until you come up to the 50 foot Harts Falls. Return back the way you came. Caution is advised for going in the winter, as ice is everywhere and makes climbing up the rocks more dangerous.

Directions
Hanover

Harts Falls

Tina Karle

Hebron Cemetery Falls

Rating 4

You are my dove hiding among the rocks on the side of a cliff. Let me see how lovely you are! Let me hear the sound of your melodious voice. Song of Solomon 2:14

Height: 4/30/50 Feet	Restrooms: No
Water: Spring/Winter	Access: Hard
Form: Tiered/Drop	Distance: ½ Mile
Coordinates: 38.50.38 N 85.22.01 W 38.50.47 N 85.22.02 W	Bench: No

Trail
Follow the coordinates to find both sets of falls. If you go to your right first in the back of the cemetery, you will see the larger falls first. There are no trails here and you must pick your own way through the brush to see these falls. After viewing the larger falls, cut across the ridge top, which is off to your right; over to the second ravine and follow the faint deer path to the next set of falls. There is an easier way down here by a large downed tree trunk. A bit of sliding is required though. Once down at the stream you can gain a lovely perspective of the falls in front of you. Rock hop your way downstream and cut across the dry ground to your right, to the other side creek coming in, and work your way up to the large downed tree section. Make your way up to your left for a nice view of the larger falls from down below. Climb up from here using rocks poking out of the ground for leverage; climbing gets much easier once you near the top. There are several nice rock ledges to climb from to gain access to the top of the hill. Follow along the top heading upstream of the large falls. You will see views of the large falls, and further upstream is a smaller cascade. Cross the creek here where the stream is much narrower and head up the slight hill back to the cemetery where a downed barbed wire fence is the place to cross back to the cemetery.

Directions
Canaan

Second Falls from the base

Large Falls

Second Falls

Hidden Falls

Rating 4

Search for wisdom as you would search for silver or hidden treasure. Then you will understand what it means to respect and to know the LORD God. Proverbs 2:4, 5

Height: 10/80 Feet	Restrooms: No
Water: Spring/Winter	Access: Moderate
Form: Cascade/Drop	Distance: ¼ Mile
Coordinates: 38.44.92 N 85.24.57 W	Bench: No

Trail

The easiest way to see these falls is to come in from Route 7. There is a park that is hidden off of Route 7, with a shelter house and picnic tables in the summer. A walk along the tree line will take you into the forest and down the slope to a side view of these lovely falls. Care MUST be taken as the drop off is quite steep and a fall can be fatal. Use common sense while walking around the cliff edge and enjoy your time here at Hidden Falls.

Directions
Madison

Ten Foot cascade

Edge of the falls

frontal view of the ten foot cascade

Top of Hidden Falls

Tina Karle

Horseshoe Falls

Rating 2

The birds of the air nest by the waters; they sing among the branches. Psalms 104:12

Height: 40 Feet	Restrooms: No
Water: Spring/Winter	Access: Hard
Form: Cascade	Distance: 1 Mile
Coordinates: 38.43.40 N 85.27.41 W	Bench: No

Trail
You will want to start off from Dead man's Falls and hike from there. Your best bet would be to get down into the creek from below and hike up the fork that will lead you to Horseshoe Falls.

Directions
Hanover

Above Horseshoe Falls

below Horseshoe falls

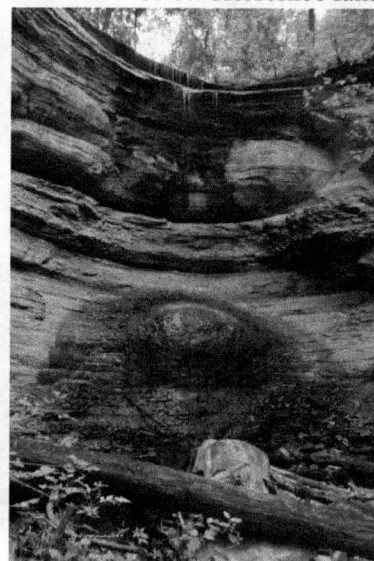

Horseshoe Falls

K Road Falls

Rating 3

Almost ethereal in its charm so beautiful, is it really there? As it plunges over the edge a fine spray of mist floats through the air. Here I stand, awed by its splendor watching its turbulent charm, as it washes down the rocks, it spreads out, and fills the creeks and rivers with its refreshing liquid.

Height: 5/10 Feet	Restrooms: No
Water: Spring/Winter	Access: Hard
Form: Cascade	Distance: Roadside-1/4th mile
Coordinates: 38.46.63 N 85.21.28W	Bench: No

Trail

From the edge of the road, cross the guardrail and walk down the slope a short ways to gain a view across the hollow of this falls. This falls runs best after a rain. Use caution if you decide to climb down into this hollow as the getting out can be tricky; especially after a rain. There is a side falls that can be seen from the other side of the hollow. This one is hidden from view unless you explore this hollow.

Directions
Madison

Upper Falls first set

second set falls

falls when dry

Main set

Side falls base

View from hillside

Rating 3

Jesus' love builds a bridge between God's heart and our deepest longings.

Height: 5 Feet	Restrooms: No
Water: Spring/Winter	Access: Easy
Form: Drop	Distance: Roadside
Coordinates: 38.52.92 N 84.52.86 W	Bench: No

Trail
From the edge of the road, cross the driveway, to gain a side view of this natural made falls turned manmade. If you gaze close enough you can see where the original ledge of the falls once was before concrete was dumped on top to create a driveway.

Directions
Norths Landing

Tina Karle

McIntyre Road Falls

Rating 3

You are my cliff to hide in, my cliff to climb. Be my safe leader, be my true mountain guide. Free me from hidden traps; I want to hide in you. I've put my life in your hands. You won't drop me, you'll never let me down. Psalms 31:3

Height: 2/5/10 Feet	Restrooms: No
Water: Spring/Winter	Access: Moderate
Form: Slide/Cascade	Distance: ½ Mile round trip
Coordinates: 38.32.99 N 85.30.14 W	Bench: No

Trail
From the road bridge, make your way down the slope to the creek. Underneath the road bridge is the first set of falls that are two feet tall. Note to your right under the cliff face a tub filled with water. Not sure if this is a spring or why it is there. Continue downstream using caution as the creek rock can be quite slippery when damp! You will find five more falls as you head downstream. Return the way you came.

Directions
New Washington

First falls under bridge

second set of falls

Third set of falls

Looking downstream

Fourth falls

Side Falls

Fifth Falls

New Prospect Cemetery Falls

Rating 4

In that day the mountains will drip new wine, and the hills will flow with milk; all the ravines of Judah will run with water. A fountain will flow out of the Lord's house and will water the valley of acacias. Joel 3:18

Height: 10/25/75 Feet	Restrooms: No
Water: Spring/Winter	Access: Hard
Form: Cascade/Drop	Distance: ½ Mile
Coordinates: Falls 1 38.39.23 N 85.27.69 W Falls 2 38.39.25 N 85.27.67 W Falls 3 38.39.25 N 85.27.59 W	Bench: No

Trail
Follow the GPS Coordinates to see these lovely falls. Use caution when seeing the largest falls from the top, as there is barbed wire strung; also, respect owner's wishes by staying only by the falls themselves.

Directions
Hanover

Upper falls first ravine

lower falls first ravine

Middle ravine

75 Foot Falls third ravine

Overhang Falls

Rating 4

Show me the path where I should go, O Lord; point out the right road for me to walk. Psalms 25: 42

Height: 5/10/30 Feet	Restrooms: No
Water: Spring/Winter	Access: Hard
Form: Drop/Cascade	Distance: 1000 Feet
Coordinates: 39.00.73 N 85.13.90 W 39.00.68 N 85.14.01W	Bench: No

Trail

From the edge of the road, make your way down the slope and head into the woods towards the creek. Follow the creek to the first two waterfalls. The last and largest set of falls requires a bushwhack to get down even with this set of falls. The hill is very steep, and the terrain slippy. Use caution when viewing the large set of falls. Return the way you came. Cross the road and walk down the concrete drainage channel. Follow the faint path along the creek to the upper set of falls.

Directions
Versailles

Fall view of falls

authors husband doing cleanup work

Winter view

First set opposite side of road

Overturf Cemetery Falls

Rating 2

The Lord is good and glad to teach the proper path to all who go astray; he will teach the ways that are right and best to those who humbly turn to Him. And when we obey Him, every path he guides u on is fragrant with His loving kindness and His truth. Psalms 25:8-10

Height: 3/10 Feet	Restrooms: No
Water: Spring/Winter	Access: Moderate
Form: Cascade/Drop	Distance: 800 Feet
Coordinates: 38.54.98 N 85.18.79 W	Bench: No

Trail
From the edge of the road, walk down the slope to see this first upper waterfall. Make your way down to the creek and walk downstream to see the last waterfall.

Directions
Canaan

Tina Karle
Pumphouse Falls

Rating 3

True intelligence is a spring of fresh water, while fools sweat it out the hard way. Proverbs 16:22

Height: 15 Feet	Restrooms: No
Water: Spring/Winter	Access: Hard
Form: Cascade	Distance: ¼ Mile
Coordinates: 38.46.31 N 85.22.76 W	Bench: No

Trail
This hike is best done in autumn through early spring. From the road, make your way down into the creek and follow said creek upstream climbing up two small falls until you reach the base of the main falls. Return back the way you came.

Directions
Madison

Quercus Grove Falls

Rating 4

I fall like a veil adorning a bride, hold on tight and enjoy the ride. Reaching the bottom I fan out feather white; smooth as silk like a birds soaring flight. Waves into ripples, streams all aglow, majestic in beauty, wild as wind is the flow. Ripples in water that stream from above, flowing southward into rivers, the majesties of love. Waters that fall filling valleys below flow into joy when the bride meets her beau.

Height: 5/15 Feet	Restrooms: No
Water: Spring/Winter	Access: Moderate
Form: Cascade	Distance: 500 Feet
Coordinates: 38.52.36 N 84.54.53 W	Bench: No

Trail
From the edge of the road, walk downstream until an easy climb can be managed to gain the creek below. Walk back upstream to the base of the falls to enjoy this hidden gem!

Directions
Quercus Grove

Driveway Falls

Main Falls

Tina Karle

Route 129 Falls

Rating 3

He waters the earth to make it fertile. The rivers of God will not run dry! He prepares the earth for His people and sends them rich harvests of grain. Psalms 65:9

Height: 3 Feet	Restrooms: No
Water: Spring/Winter	Access: Moderate
Form: Cascade	Distance: 500 Feet
Coordinates: 39.01.49 N 85.14.23 W	Bench: No

Trail

From the edge of the road, make your way down the slippery hill, and jump across the concrete drainage channel into the woods. Walk over to the edge of the creek to see this falls.

Directions
Versailles

Rating 4

As I hike down the wooded path, dappled with the suns yellow beams shining through the towering trees, a small clearing comes into view. A beacon seems to be shining down an amazing sight yet found, for few have yet to travel here. Its beauty not yet tainted. Tread lightly over to the edge to be awed to silence by the sound; of the powerful untamed waterfall, that's plunging and cascading down; to crash upon the rocks below.

Height: 10/70 Feet	Restrooms: No
Water: Spring/Winter	Access: Hard
Form: Cascade/Drop	Distance: ½ Mile
Coordinates: 38.42.29 N 85.28.24 W	Bench: No

Trail

From the schoolyard walk along the edge of the woods until you come upon the obvious trail. Take the first creek bridge and follow the well beaten path towards the high school. The path will meander then towards the right back into the woods. The path becomes faint in some spots but continue heading towards your right until you come upon the creek. Follow the creek down and you will find the upper tucked away falls and a side falls that is normally dry. Follow down to the base of the dry falls and continue following the path. It will lead you right to the base of the next cascading falls. Use caution here as a fall could be fatal. You will also notice the mysterious ledge that leads to the 70 foot larger falls. Continue following the trail to your left along the cliff edge. This IS not for the faint of heart as this trail follows right next to the edge of the cliff. Once past the cliff the trail turns a sharp right and tucks back under the cliff edge you just walked along. Follow this along until the view of the falls comes up. Use extreme caution if you so choose to try for the base of the falls. It is slippery and can be difficult getting to the bottom. I had my husband to hold onto going down that steep hillside. It is best to not come here alone as a fall would be fatal. Return the way you came to the falls.

Directions
Hanover

Ledge view of falls

Base view of falls

Upper first falls

Down creek view

Middle set of falls

Early spring view

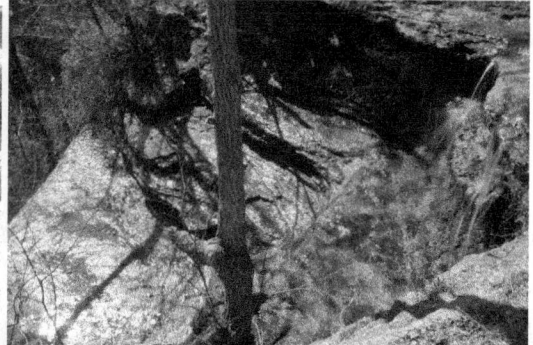

view of both sets of falls

Edge of both falls from top

Dry Falls

Zion Cemetery Falls

Rating 2

I'm sending my Angel ahead of you to guard you in your travels, to lead you to the place that I've prepared. Exodus 23:20

Height: 6 Feet	Restrooms: No
Water: Spring/Winter	Access: Hard
Form: Cascade	Distance: ½ Mile
Coordinates: 38.37.83 N 85.29.03 W	Bench: No

Trail

From the cemetery make your way to the left skirting the farmer's field, staying IN THE WOODS; make your way through the tangled underbrush and msc sticker bushes down to the creek. Follow the creek downstream until you come to the falls. This creek is a fooler as there was to be a large falls here and after scouting the entire creek, past the six foot falls, there isn't much to be found accept a side falls. This is a nice creek to explore though. Watch out for ticks.

Directions
Saluda

Side Falls downstream

main falls

Small cascade along the way

Mini Waterfalls

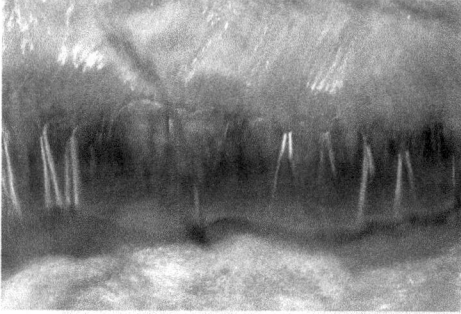

300 S Road Falls

Rating 2

They gave water for all the animals to drink. There the wild donkeys quench their thirst, and the birds nest beside the streams and sing among the branches of the trees. Psalms 104:11,12

Height: 2 Feet	Restrooms: No
Water: Spring/Winter	Access: Easy
Form: Drop	Distance: Roadside
Coordinates: 39.01.84 N 85.10.16 W	Bench: No

Trail
From the edge of the road, carefully make your way down the slope to the creeks edge to view this petite waterfall.

Directions
From downtown Madison take Route 421 going north for 25.1 miles. Turn right onto US 50. Drive about 5.3 miles. Turn right onto S County Road 525 and drive 1.7 miles. Turn right at S Friendship Road and drive .1 miles. Continue onto 300 S County Road and drive about .1 miles to the falls.

Tina Karle

650 S Road Falls

Rating 2

The streams of God's kindness continuously wash over us and fill our hearts with joy.

Height: 3 Feet	Restrooms: No
Water: Spring/Winter	Access: Easy
Form: Cascade	Distance: Roadside
Coordinates: 38.58.65 N 85.10.37 W	Bench: No

Trail
From the edge of the road, walk through the brush to the creeks edge to see this set of falls.

Directions
From the town of Versailles take N Washington Street heading south toward Tyson Street. Take the first right onto Tyson Street. Take the first left onto N Adams Street. Turn left onto Route 129 and drive 5.7 miles. Turn left at Olean Road and drive 3.5 miles. Take a sharp right onto E County Road 650 S and follow this dead end road about .6 miles to the falls located on your left.

Barkworks Road Falls

Rating 2

He'll take charge of sending the rain at the right time, both autumn and spring rains, so that you'll be able to harvest your grain, your grapes, and your olives. Deuteronomy 11:13

Height: 2 Feet	Restrooms: No
Water: Spring/Winter	Access: Moderate
Form: Cascade	Distance: Roadside
Coordinates: 38.52.26 N 84.54.58 W	Bench: No

Trail
From the edge of the road, find the easiest path to get down to the creek to view this set of falls.

Directions
From Patriot take Route 250 going west for six miles. Take a slight right onto Quercus Grove Road/Barkworks Road and drive about one and a half miles to the first set of falls located on your left.

Bear Branch Falls

Rating 2

For He draws up the drops of water, they distill rain from the mist, which the clouds pour down, they drip upon man abundantly. Job 36:27, 28

Height: 2 Feet	Restrooms: No
Water: Spring/Winter	Access: Easy
Form: Cascade	Distance: Roadside
Coordinates: 38.54.78 N 85.06.75 W	Bench: No

Trail

From the edge of the road, make your way over to the creeks edge to see these small set of falls!

Directions

From downtown Madison take Route 421 going north for 6.9 miles. Turn right onto Route 250 and drive six miles to Route 62. Turn left onto Route 62 and continue driving through Canaan to stay on Route 62. Drive about 7.8 miles until you come to Route 129. Turn right onto Route 129 and drive 2.2 miles until you come to Pleasant Grove Road. Turn left and drive .4 miles. Turn left at Aaron Road and drive .8 miles. Take a slight left at Knigga Road and drive 1.4 miles. Continue onto Aberdeen Road and drive 1.4 miles. Turn right to stay on Aberdeen Road and continue another 1.1 miles. Continue to stay on Aberdeen road after turning right and go another .8 miles. Take the third left onto Bear Valley Drive and follow to almost the end of the road to the falls, which are on the right hand side.

Bear Creek Falls

Rating 4

At your command the springs burst forth to give your people water; and then you dried a path for them across the ever flowing Jordan. Psalms 74:15

Height: 2 Feet	Restrooms: No
Water: Spring/Winter	Access: Moderate
Form: Cascade	Distance: Roadside
Coordinates: 38.55.28 N 85.08.62 W	Bench: No

Trail
From the road ford, look upstream to see the cascading set of falls. You do NOT have to cross this ford if you don't have to. But good water boots are a must to see the falls.

Directions
Head north on Route 421 16.5 miles. Turn right at W County Road 800 South and drive 6.7 miles. Turn right at Route 129 and drive one mile. Turn left at E County Road 900 S and drive .8 miles. Turn right at County Road 375 E and drive a half mile. Continue onto E County Road 950 S. Turn right at S County Road 450 E and drive a half a mile. Take the first left onto County Road 1000 S. Continue onto Bear Creek Road. Turn left at Iceberg Road and drive about 1.7 miles to the creek ford.

Tina Karle

Bee Camp Creek

Rating 2

The deep fountains of the earth were broken open by His knowledge, and the skies poured down rain.
Proverbs 3:20

Height: 2 Feet	Restrooms: No
Water: Spring/Winter	Access: Easy
Form: Cascade	Distance: Roadside
Coordinates: 38.45.20 N 85.17.92 W	Bench: No

Trail
From the edge of the road, walk over to the creeks edge to view this set of falls.

Directions
From Madison take Route 56 heading east for 4.6 miles. Turn left onto Bee Camp Road. Drive .7 miles to the falls located on the left hand side. Pull off so as not to block traffic to view this set of falls.

Boyd Branch Falls

Rating 2

But the land you are about to cross the river and take for your own is a land of mountains and valleys; it drinks water that rains from the sky. It's a land that God, your God, personally tends-He's the gardener-He alone keeps His eye on it all year long. Deuteronomy 11:10

Height: 2 Feet	Restrooms: No
Water: Year	Access: Easy
Form: Cascade	Distance: Roadside
Coordinates: 38.59.20 N 85.05.09 W	Bench: No

Trail
From the edge of the road you can view these cascading falls as you drive down the no outlet road. Respect homeowner's privacy and enjoy the short drive!

Directions
Head north on Route 421 for 16.5 miles. Turn right at W County Road 800 S and drive 6.7 miles. Continue straight onto Route 62 and go 2.5 miles. Turn left to stay on Route 62 and go 1.1 miles. Turn right to stay on Route 62 driving .4 miles. Turn right again to stay on Route 62 for .3 miles. Take the first right onto Route 62 for 4.3 miles. Turn left at Pruss Road and drive up the road about .18 of a mile to see the first set of falls.

Tina Karle

County Road 275 Falls

Rating 2

When they walk through the Valley of Weeping it will become a place of springs where pools of blessing and refreshment collect after rain! Psalms 84:6

Height: 3 Feet	Restrooms: No
Water: Spring/Winter	Access: Moderate
Form: Drop	Distance: Roadside
Coordinates: 38.54.98N 85.18.79 W	Bench: No

Trail
From the edge of the road, walk into the woods and make your way down the slope towards the creek. You will have to walk past the falls to make your way down the small slope to the creek. Walk up the creek a short ways to see this set of falls.

Directions
From Madison take Route 421 going north for 13.1 miles. Turn right at W County Road 1050 S and drive 1.2 miles. Turn left at S County Road 450 W and drive 230 feet. Turn right onto W County Road 1025 S and drive one mile. Turn right to stay on County Road 1025. Continue onto S County Road 275 and drive about .7 miles, passing Overturf Cemetery Falls along the way. Pull off to the side of the road.

County Road 650 S Falls

Rating 2

I will pour out water for the thirsty land and make streams flow on dry land. Isaiah 44:3

Height: 3 Feet	Restrooms: No
Water: Spring/Winter	Access: Easy
Form: Cascade	Distance: Roadside
Coordinates: 38.58.85 N 85.13.20 W	Bench: No

Trail
From the edge of the road, make your way through the woods to see this pretty set of falls.

Directions
From downtown Versailles take N Washington Street heading south. Take the first right onto Tyson Street. Take the first left onto N Adams Street. Turn left onto Route 129 and drive 6.2 miles. Turn right at E County Road 650 S and drive .18 of a mile and pull off the side of the road. The falls will be on your left.

Tina Karle

County Road 40 Falls

Rating 2

They wind through lonesome valleys, come upon brooks, discover cool springs and pools brimming with rain! Psalms 84:5

Height: 4 Feet	Restrooms: No
Water: Spring/Winter	Access: Easy
Form: Slide	Distance: Roadside
Coordinates: 38.59.38 N 85.35.94 W	Bench: No

Trail

From the edge of the road, make your way through the woods to the creeks edge to view these slanted falls. Use the above coordinates to exactly find where these hidden falls are located at along County Road. At the beginning of County Road there is another set of falls that are close to the edge of the road down the hillside close to where the creek flows towards Muscatatuk River.

Directions

In North Vernon on Route 3/7 head south for 1.5 miles till you come to Ripley Street. Turn left onto Ripley Street. Continue onto E County Road 20 N. E County Road 20 N becomes E County Road 40 N. Drive about .18 of a mile to see the falls off to your right. They can be hard to find at times if they are not running. They blend into the surrounding woods quite well!

Dry Fork Road Falls

Rating 2

Your pathway led through the sea, a path no one knew was there! Psalms 77:19

Height: 2 Feet	Restrooms: No
Water: Spring/Winter	Access: Easy
Form: Cascade	Distance: Roadside
Coordinates: 38.47.68 N 85.11.66 W	Bench: No

Trail
From the edge of the road, walk down to the creek to see this cascade set of falls.

Directions
From Madison, take Route 56 going east for 7.4 miles. Turn left at Brooksburg Street and go .2 miles. Turn left at Brooksburg Back Street and go .1 mile.

Tina Karle

Hard Scrabble Road Falls

Rating 2

The wild animals in the fields will thank Me, the jackals and ostriches to, for giving them water in the wilderness, yes, springs in the desert, so that my people, my chosen ones, can be refreshed. Isaiah 43:20

Height: 2 Feet	Restrooms: No
Water: Spring/Winter	Access: Easy
Form: Cascade	Distance: Roadside
Coordinates: 38.44.86 N 85.18.19 W	Bench: No

Trail
From the edge of the road, walk through the woods to see this set of falls.

Directions
From downtown Madison take Route 56 going east for 4 miles. Turn left at Bee Camp Road and drive .4 miles. Take the first left onto Hard Scrabble Road and drive watching to your left for two different sets of falls. Pull over to the edge of the road to see these falls.

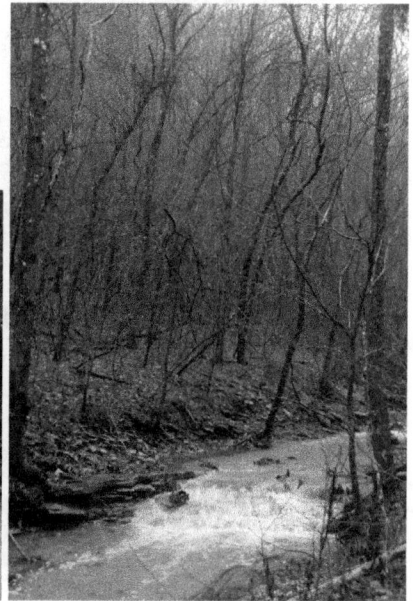

Horton Hollow Falls

Rating 1

I will lead them to streams of water. They will walk on a level road and not stumble. Jeremiah 31:9

Height: 3 Feet	Restrooms: No
Water: Spring/Winter	Access: Easy
Form: Cascade	Distance: Roadside
Coordinates: 38.52.61 N 85.14.63 W	Bench: No

Trail
From the edge of the road as you drive up Horton Hollow watch for these cascading falls.

Directions
From Madison, head north on Route 421 for 7.3 miles. Turn right onto Route 250 and drive .6 miles. Continue to stay on Route 250 as it makes its many turns. Shortly Route 250 joins with Route 62. Turn right onto Route 250 where they separate. Drive up the hill watching the small creek on your right as you go. The falls will be along the road in about .4 miles. You will pass another waterfall right as you turn onto Route 250. There is a small pull off to enjoy Wilson Fork Falls.

Tina Karle

Iceberg Road Falls

Rating 2

God will provide rain for the seeds you sow. The grain that grows will be abundant. Your cattle will range far and wide. Oblivious to war and earthquake, the oxen and donkeys you use for hauling and plowing will be fed well near running brooks that flow freely from mountains and hills. Isaiah 30:23

Height: 3 Feet	Restrooms: No
Water: Spring/Winter	Access: Easy
Form: Cascade	Distance: Roadside
Coordinates: 38.55.42 N 85.09.48 W	Bench: No

Trail
Respect homeowner's privacy and hop out to only view the falls. Leave only footprints, take only pictures.

Directions
From Madison, take Route 421 going north for 16.5 miles. Turn right onto County Road 800 S and drive 6.7 miles. Turn right onto Route 129/62 and drive one mile. Turn left at E County Road 900 and drive .8 miles. Turn right onto County Road 375 and drive a half mile. Continue onto County Road 950. Turn right onto County Road 450 and drive a half a mile. Take the first left onto County Road 1000. Continue onto Bear Creek Road. Turn left at Iceberg Road and drive .6 miles to see the falls on your right.

Iceberg Road Falls upper

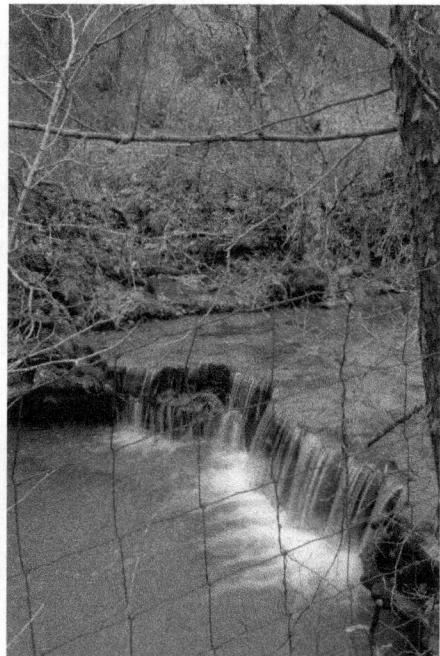

Lower Falls

Indian Creek Falls

Rating 2

For I will pour water on the thirsty ground and send streams coursing through the parched earth. I will pour my Spirit into your descendants and my blessing on your children. They shall sprout like grass on the prairie, like willows alongside creeks. Isaiah 44:1

Height: 2 Feet	Restrooms: No
Water: Year	Access: Easy
Form: Drop	Distance: 200 Feet
Coordinates: 38.48.40 N 85.06.50 W	Bench: No

Trail
From the edge of the road make your way past the barbed fence that is pushed down to the edge of the small cliff. From here you can see the side view of this set of falls.

Directions
In Madison take Route 56 going east for 19.8 miles. Turn left at Ferry Street and go .3 miles. Turn right onto Route 56 and go 3.6 miles. Continue onto Bennington Pike for 2.3 miles. Turn right at Cole Road and go .1 miles to the falls located on your right.

Tina Karle

Indian Kentuck Creek Falls

Rating 3

I am the Lord, who opens a way through the waters, making a path right through the sea. Isaiah 43:16

Height: 2 Feet	Restrooms: No
Water: Year	Access: Easy
Form: Cascade	Distance: Roadside
Coordinates: 38.53.55 N 85.17.13 W	Bench: No

Trail
From the edge of the road you can view this petite set of cascading falls. You might even want to try your hand at fishing here too!

Directions
Head north on Route 421 from downtown Madison. Drive 7.3 miles and turn right onto Route 250 and continue for .6 miles. Take the first right onto Route 250 and drive 5.8 miles. Take the first left onto Barbersville Road and drive 1.7 miles. Turn left at Barbersville Creek Road and drive .7 miles. Take the slight left onto Bloody Run Road and pull off there by the edge of the road. Falls are to your left.

Rating 3

We glide along the tides of time as swiftly as a racing river, and vanish as quickly as a dream. Psalms 90:5

Height: 3 Feet	Restrooms: No
Water: Spring/Winter	Access: Easy
Form: Cascade	Distance: Roadside
Coordinates: 38.48.38N 85.14.22 W	Bench: No

Trail
From the edge of the road, make your way into the trees to the creeks edge to see this cascading set of falls! A nice little respite as you are driving along this rocky road!

Directions
From downtown Madison go north on Route 421 3.3 miles. Turn right onto Route 62 and drive 3.8 miles. Continue onto N China Mainville Road and drive 4.4 miles. Turn left at Brushy Fork Road and dive 3.1 miles. Turn right at County Road 480/E Little Brushy Fork Road and drive less than .1 of a mile to the falls located on the right.

Tina Karle

Little Creek Falls

Rating 3

The Lord is my strength and my song. Exodus 15:2

Height: 3 Feet	Restrooms: No
Water: Spring/Winter	Access: Easy
Form: Cascade	Distance: Roadside
Coordinates: 38.55.96 N 85.07.88 W	Bench: No

Trail
From the edge of the road, make your way upstream to see these cascading falls!

Directions
From Versailles turn left onto Route 129 and drive 8.1 miles. Turn left at Route 62 and drive 2.5 miles. Turn right at S County Road 525 E and drive a half mile. Turn left at E County Road 900 S and go 1.4 miles. Turn right at S Bear Creek Road and go .7 miles and turn right again to stay on Bear Creek Road. Drive 1.2 miles to the falls located on your right hand side.

Long Road Falls

Rating 2

It is God who arms me with strength and makes my way perfect. Psalms 18:32

Height: 2 Feet	Restrooms: No
Water: Spring/Winter	Access: Easy
Form: Cascade	Distance: Roadside
Coordinates: 38.45.03 N 85.09.81 W	Bench: No

Trail
From the edge of the road make your way over to the edge to see these falls. Or you can pick your way down the slope to the creek bottom to gain a different view of the falls.

Directions
From downtown Vevay take Route 56 going west to Route 129. Turn left or north onto Route 129. Drive 2.3 miles and turn left onto Long Run Road. Drive 2.8 miles along Long Run Road to the main falls. You will pass two other small falls along the way. Further up from the main falls is another small falls as well.

Mennets Hollow

Rating 2

O God, you are my God, earnestly I seek you; my soul thirsts for you, my body longs for you, in a dry and weary land where there is no water. Psalms 63:1

Height: 3 Feet	Restrooms: No
Water: Spring/Winter	Access: Easy
Form: Cascade	Distance: Roadside
Coordinates: 38.44.68 N 85.08.54 W	Bench: No

Trail

From the edge of the road, make your way over to the edge of the hill to see these falls. To gain a frontal view of the falls, carefully pick your way down the hill to the creeks edge to see this pretty falls. Use caution after a heavy rain as the current can become quite strong.

Directions

From downtown Vevay take Route 56 going west to Route 129. Turn right onto Route 129 and drive 2.3 miles. Turn left onto Long Run Road and drive 1.6 miles. Turn left onto Mennets Hollow Road and drive about .2 miles to the falls located on your right.

Pendleton Run Falls

Rating 2

The Lord gives me strength. He makes my feet as sure as those of a deer, and he helps me stand on the mountains. Habakuk 3:19

Height: 2 Feet	Restrooms: No
Water: Spring/Winter	Access: Easy
Form: Cascade	Distance: Roadside
Coordinates: 38.46.32 N 85.07.26 W	Bench: No

Trail
From the edge of the road, walk over to the creek to view this set of falls! There is along the way to the main falls, a fake set of falls right as you cross the road bridge. This looks like it would be a great spot for swimming and fishing during summers limpid heat!

Directions
From Vevay on Route 56, turn right or north onto Route 129. Drive 1.2 miles and turn right onto Jackson Road and drive .8 miles. Take a slight left onto Pendleton Run Road and drive about 1.6 miles to the falls which will be located on your left.

Bridge fake falls

Main Falls

Tina Karle

Peter Creek

Rating 2

Pile your troubles on God's shoulders. He'll carry your load, He'll help you out. He'll never let good people topple into ruin. Psalms 55:22

Height: 2 Feet	Restrooms: No
Water: Spring/Winter	Access: Easy
Form: Tier/Cascade	Distance: Roadside
Coordinates: 39.00.43 N 85.05.14 W 39.00.42 N 85.05.19 W	Bench: No

Trail
From the edge of the road, walk into the woods to the creeks edge to view these falls.

Directions
From downtown Dillsboro turn left onto Sunset Drive and drive a half mile. Continue onto Sunset Drive and drive another half mile. Turn right onto Sangamaw Road and drive another half mile to the falls located on your right.

Raccoon Creek Falls

Rating 2

The parched ground will become a pool, with springs of water in the thirsty land. Where desert jackals lived, there will be reeds and rushes! Isaiah 35:7

Height: 2 Feet	Restrooms: No
Water: Spring/Winter	Access: Easy
Form: Cascade	Distance: Roadside
Coordinates: 38.59.05 N 85.12.88 W	Bench: No

Trail
From the parking lot, make your way through the small woods to the creeks edge to view these cascading falls.

Directions
Head north on Route 421 from downtown Madison. You will drive 16.4 miles and make a right onto County road 800 S. Drive 6.7 miles and turn left onto Route 129. Drive 1.7 miles and turn right onto County Road 650 S and follow down to the end.

Tina Karle

Route 262 Falls

Rating 2

You let me rest in fields of green grass. You lead me to streams of peaceful water. Psalms 23:2

Height: 2 Feet	Restrooms: No
Water: Spring/Winter	Access: Easy
Form: Cascade	Distance: Roadside
Coordinates: 38.56.39 N 84.56.04 W	Bench: No

Trail
From the edge of the road, walk over to the creeks edge to view this cascading falls.

Directions
From downtown Rising Sun turn west onto Route 262. Follow Route 262 for about 4.6 miles to the falls located on your left.

Salem Branch Falls

Rating 2

It's like a grove of palm trees or a garden beside a river. You are like tall aloe trees that the Lord has planted, or like cedars growing near water. Numbers 24:6

Height: 3 Feet	Restrooms: No
Water: Spring/Winter	Access: Easy
Form: Cascade	Distance: Roadside
Coordinates: 38.54.76 N 85.12.81 W	Bench: No

Trail
From the edge of the road, carefully make your way down the steep slope to see the first set of falls. Climb up the bank, bypassing the falls and make your way upstream to see the next set of cascading falls.

Directions
In Versailles take Route 421 to Route 129. Drive south along Route 129 for 10.5 miles. Turn right onto Route 62 and drive about 1.4 miles to the falls located on your right.

Lower Set of falls

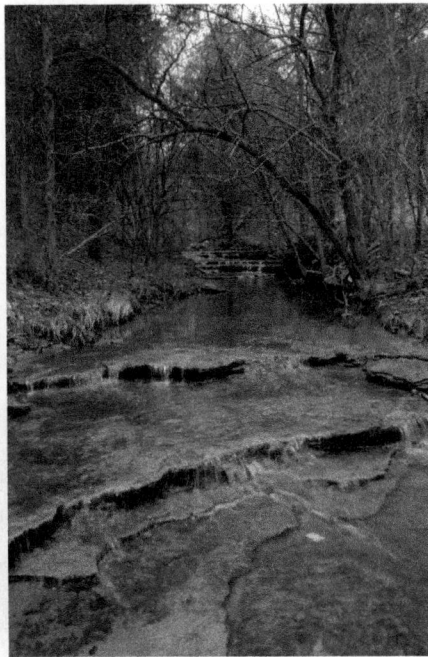

Upper Set of falls

South Fork Falls

Rating 3

The wild animals honor me, the jackals and the owls, because I provide water in the wilderness and streams in the wasteland, to give drink to my people, my chosen. Isaiah 43:20

Height: 2 Feet	Restrooms: No
Water: Year	Access: Easy
Form: Cascade	Distance: Roadside
Coordinates: 38.54.93 N 85.02.88 W	Bench: No

Trail
From the edge of the road, walk over to the creek's edge to see this petite set of falls.

Directions
From Rising Sun, go south on Route 56 along the Ohio River. Turn right to stay on Route 56 and drive 6.7 miles. Continue onto Aberdeen Road for 3.8 miles. Turn right at Goodner Road and go less than .1 miles to the falls located on your right.

Tate Ridge Road Falls

Rating 2

The advice of a wise man refreshes like water from a mountain spring. Those accepting it become aware of the pitfalls on ahead. Proverbs 13:14

Height: 2 Feet	Restrooms: No
Water: Spring/Winter	Access: Easy
Form: Cascade	Distance: Roadside
Coordinates: 38.48.38 N 85.14.22 W	Bench: No

Trail
From the edge of the road walk through the woods to the creek to view these falls.

Directions
From Madison drive north on Route 421 for 3.3 miles. Turn right onto Route 62 and go 3.8 miles. Continue onto N China/Mainville Road and drive 4.4 miles. Turn left at E Brushy Fork Road and drive 4.2 miles. Take a slight right onto E Tate Ridge Road and go .1 miles to the falls.

Toddy's Creek Falls

Rating 2

They longed for me to speak as they longed for rain. They waited eagerly, for my words were as refreshing as the spring rain. Job 29:23

Height: 2 Feet	Restrooms: No
Water: Year	Access: Easy
Form: Cascade	Distance: Roadside
Coordinates: 38.51.18 N 85.20.30 W	Bench: No

Trail
Form the edge of the road look upstream and you can see these lovely falls!

Directions
From Madison, go north on Route 421. Take the S 250 road to your right. Turn left onto N Graham Road. Follow this road for .1 mile and turn right onto S-250. Follow S-250 crossing over the West Fork creek and then continuing on, you will cross over Toddy's Branch two times before you come to the falls a bit further up the road on your left.

Rating 2

They give water to all the beasts of the field; the wild donkeys quench their thirst. The birds of the sky nest by the waters; they sing among the branches. Psalms 104:11, 12

Height: 2 Feet	Restrooms: No
Water: Spring/Winter	Access: Easy
Form: Cascade	Distance: Roadside
Coordinates: 38.48.87 N 85.17.54 W 38.48.64 N 85.17.91 W	Bench: No

Trail
From the edge of the road walk over to the creek to see the cascading falls at both locations!

Directions
From Madison take Route 421 north for 3.3 miles. Turn right onto Route 62 and drive 3.8 miles. Continue onto China/Mainville Road and drive 2.6 miles. Turn left onto N Turkey Branch Road and go about .5 miles to the falls. Continue down the road to view the next set on the right.

Tina Karle
Uhlman Creek Falls

Rating 2

He split rocks in the wilderness, gave them all they could drink from underground springs; He made creeks flow out from sheer rock, and water pour out like a river. Psalms 78:9

Height: 3 Feet	Restrooms: No
Water: Spring/Winter	Access: Easy
Form: Cascade	Distance: Roadside
Coordinates: 38.53.82 N 85.10.65 W	Bench: No

Trail
Please respect homeowner's privacy! Stop to view these falls and snap a picture for posterity and then be on your way!! Leave only footprints take only pictures….

Directions
From downtown Madison take Route 421 going north for 6.9 miles. Turn right onto route 250 and follow Route 250 through many turns for 13.8 miles. When you come to Route 129 turn right and drive 2.2 miles. Turn left onto Pleasant Grove Road and drive .3 miles. Turn left at Levi Bliss Road and drive .2 miles to the falls located on your right.

Waterloo Road Falls

Rating 2

The lame man will leap up like a deer, and those who could not speak will shout and sing! Springs will burst forth in the wilderness, and streams in the desert. Isaiah 35:6

Height: 3 Feet	Restrooms: No
Water: Spring/Winter	Access: Moderate
Form: Cascade	Distance: Roadside
Coordinates: 38.54.77 N 85.10.97 W	Bench: No

Trail
Make your way through the woods to the creeks edge to view these petite falls!

Directions
From downtown Madison take Route 421 going north for 6.9 miles. Turn right onto route 250 and follow Route 250 through many turns for 13.8 miles. When you come to Route 129 turn right and drive .6 miles. Take the second left onto Waterloo Road and drive 1 mile to the falls located on your right.

West Fork Falls

Rating 2

Height: 2 Feet	Restrooms: No
Water: Year	Access: Easy
Form: Cascade	Distance: Roadside
Coordinates: 38.49.24 N 85.19.81 W	Bench: No

Trail
From the edge of the road, walk over to the edge to view these petite falls. Note: when the creek is up the falls will be hidden from view.

Directions
From Route 421 turn east onto Route 250. Turn left then right and go down to the bottom of the hill. Turn a quick right keeping the creek to your left. Go through the town of China and turn left onto China Manville Road. In less than a half mile on your right, watch for the tiny falls. Pull off into the grass to see the falls.

Wolf Run

Rating 2

But my brothers are fickle as a gulch in the desert— one day they're gushing with water
from melting ice and snow cascading out of the mountains, but by midsummer they're dry, gullies baked dry
in the sun. Job 6:14

Height: 3 Feet	Restrooms: No
Water: Spring/Winter	Access: Easy
Form: Cascade	Distance: Roadside
Coordinates: 38.46.38 N 85.18.89 W	Bench: No

Trail
From the edge of the road, look upstream to see this cascading set of falls.

Directions
From downtown Madison turn north onto Route 421 and drive .6 miles. Turn right onto Aulenbach Avenue
and drive two miles. Aulenbach Avenue turns into Dugan Hollow Road. Dugan Hollow Road turns slightly
left and becomes County Road 133/N Rykers Ridge Road. Drive another 1.3 miles. Continue onto E Wolf
Run Road and drive about one mile to the falls located on your left.

Tina Karle

Bibliography

McKinney, Sally *Hiking Indiana,* Versa Press, 2000

McPherson, Alan, *Paddle Indiana-An Access Guide to Canoeing & Kayaking Indian's Lakes & Streams,* J.L. Waters & Co.inc. Bloomington, IN, 2000

McPherson, Alan, *Nature Walks in Southern Indiana,* Hoosier Chapter of the Sierra Club, Indianapolis, IN, 1995

McPherson, Alan, *Nature Walks in Southern Indiana, Revised & Expanded 2nd Edition,* Waters Publishing Co, Bloomington, IN, 2002

Other Resources

AmericanWhiteWater-www.americanwhitewater.org
Bing Maps www.bingmaps.com
Topography Maps-www.mytopo.com
Geocaching Website-www.Geocaching.com
Map Directions-www.mapquest.com/www.googlemaps.com
Topography Maps-www.topomaker.com

Waterfalls By Area

Bascom Corner

Bascom Corner Falls	96
White Road Falls	93

Bear Branch

Aberdeen Road Falls	24
Bear Branch Falls	136
Bear Creek Falls	137
Bear Valley Road Falls	97
Iceberg Road Falls	146
Little Creek Falls	150
One Lane Road Falls	76
Salem Branch Falls	157
Uhlman Creek Falls	162
Waterloo Road Falls	163

Bryantsburg

Alcove Falls	25
Barking Dog Falls	95
Camp Meeting Road Falls	35
County Road 050 Falls	100
E 1033 Road Falls	108
Indian Kentuck Cemetery	63
Indian Kentuck Creek Falls	148
Thornton Road Falls	89

Canaan

County Road 275 Falls	140
Deer Path Falls	50
Hebron Cemetery Falls	112
Horton hollow Falls	145
Overturf Cemetery Falls	125
Toddy's Creek Falls	160

China

Dry Fork Creek	52
Little Brushy Fork	149
Route 62 Falls	81
Sweet Water Road Falls	88
Tate Ridge Road Falls	159
Turkey Run	161
West Fork Falls	164

Dillsboro

Arnold Creek Falls	26
Boyd Branch Falls	139
Farmers Retreat Falls	55
Peter Creek	154

Hanover

Butler Falls	30
Chain Mill Falls	36
Crowe Falls	104
Deadmans Falls	48
Fremont Falls	109
Hanover Beach Hill Falls	58
Harts Falls	110
Horseshoe Falls	116
London Road Falls	67
Lowry Lane Falls	69
Lucina Ball Drive Falls	70
New Prospect Cemetery	122
Scenic Drive Falls	83
Schoolhouse Falls	129
Tull Road Falls	91

Madison

Bee Camp Creek	138
Clifty Falls	37
Cragmont Street Falls	101
Crooked Creek Falls	45
Crooked Creek Main Falls	103
Dry Falls	51
Dugan Hollow Falls	106
Dugan Hollow Road Falls	39
Eagle Hollow Falls	54
Hanging Rock Falls	57
Hard Scrabble Road Falls	144
Hatcher Hill Falls	60
Hidden Falls	114
K Road Falls	117
Michigan Road Falls	71
Old State Route 62	74
Pumphouse Falls	126
Route 7 Falls	78
Route 56 Falls	80
Route 421 Falls	82
Sunrise Golf Course	85
Vulture Falls	92
Wolf Run	165

North Vernon

Brushy Creek Falls	28
County Road 40 Falls	142
County Road 325 Falls	99
Huckleberry Branch Falls	62
Muscatatuck County Park	72

Olean

650 S Road Falls	134
County Road 650 S Falls	141
Olean Cemetery Falls	75
Raccoon Creek Falls	155

Quercus Grove

Barkworks Road Falls	135
Brown Road Falls	27
Quercus Grove Falls	127

Rising Sun

Route 262 Falls	156
South Fork Falls	158

Saluda

Bull Creek Falls	29
Camp Creek Falls	34
Dobson Hollow Falls	106
Little Bull Creek Falls	65
McIntyre Road Falls	120
Zion Cemetery Falls	131

Vernon

Cali Nature Preserve	32
County Road 125 S Falls	98
Crosley Lake Falls	46
Route 3 Falls	77

Versailles

300 S Falls	133
Overhang Falls	124
Route 129 Falls	128
Signor Hill Road Falls	84

Vevay

Dry Fork Road Falls	143
Long Branch Falls	119
Long Run Falls	151
Lost Fork Road Falls	68
Mennets Hollow	152
Pendleton Run Falls	153

Index

A

Aberdeen Road Falls	24
Alcove Falls	25
Arnold Creek Falls	26

B

Barking Dog Falls	95
Bascom Corner Falls	96
Barkworks Road Falls	135
Bear Branch Falls	136
Bear Creek Falls	137
Bear Valley Road Falls	97
Bee Camp Creek	138
Boyd Branch Falls	139
Brown Road Falls	27
Brushy Creek Falls	28
Bull Creek Falls	29
Butler Falls	30

C

Cali Nature Preserve	32
Camp Creek Falls	34
Camp Meeting Road Falls	35
Chain Mill Falls	36
Clifty Falls	37
County Road 125 S	98
County Road 40 Falls	142
County Road 275 Falls	140
County Road 325 Falls	99
County Road 650 S Falls	141
County Road 950 Falls	100
Cragmont Street Falls	101
Crooked Creek Falls	45
Crooked Creek Main Falls	103
Crosley Lake Falls	46
Crowe Falls	104

D

Deadmans Falls	48
Deer Path Falls	50
Dobson Hollow Falls	106
Dry Falls	51
Dry Fork Creek	52
Dry Fork Road Falls	143
Dugan Hollow Falls	106
Dugan Hollow Road Falls	39

E

E 1033 Road Falls	108
Eagle Hollow Falls	54

F

Farmers Retreat Falls	55
Fremont Falls	109

H

Hanging Rock Falls	57
Hanover Beach Hill Falls	58
Hard Scrabble Road Falls	144
Harts Falls	110
Hatcher Hill Falls	60
Hebron Cemetery Falls	112
Hidden Falls	114
Horton Hollow Falls	145
Horseshoe Falls	116
Huckleberry Branch Falls	62

I

Iceberg Road Falls	146
Indian Creek Falls	147
Indian Kentuck Cemetery	63
Indian Kentuck Creek Falls	148

K

K Road Falls	117

L

Little Brushy Fork	149
Little Bull Creek Falls	65
Little Creek Falls	150
London Road Falls	67
Long Branch Falls	119
Long Run Falls	151
Lost Fork Road Falls	68
Lowry Lane Falls	69
Lucina Ball Drive Falls	70

M

McIntyre Road Falls	120
Mennets Hollow	152
Michigan Road Falls	71
Muscatatuk County Falls	72

N

New Prospect Cemetery 122

O

Old State Route 62 74
Olean Cemetery Falls 75
One Lane Road Falls 76
Overhang Falls 124
Overturf Cemetery Falls 125

P

Pendelton Run Falls 153
Peter Creek 154
Pumphouse Falls 126

Q

Quercus Grove Falls 127

R

Raccoon Creek Falls 155
Route 3 Falls 77
Route 7 Falls 78
Route 56 Falls 80
Route 62 Falls 81
Route 129 Falls 128
Route 262 Falls 156
Route 421 Falls 82

S

Salem Branch Falls 157
Scenic Drive Falls 83
Schoolhouse Falls 129
Signor Hill Road Falls 84
South Fork Falls 158
Sunrise Golf Course 85
Sweet Water Road Falls 88

T

Tate Ridge Road Falls 159
Thornton Road Falls 89
Toddy's Creek Falls 160
Tull Road Falls 91
Turkey Run 161

U

Uhlman Creek Falls 162

V

Vulture Falls 92

W

Waterloo Road Falls 163
West Fork Falls 164
White Road Falls 93
Wolf Run 165

Z

Zion Cemetery Falls 131

300S Road Falls 133
650 S Road Falls 134

About the Author

Tina Karle, author of *Falling Waters of Ohio (109 Hikeable Falls in Ohio), Falling Waters of Ohio; a coffee table book, 200 Waterfall Hikes in Ohio, Celebration of Flowers,120 Waterfall Hikes Around Cincinnati Ohio, and 70 Waterfall Hikes of Dayton,* was born and raised in Ohio. Her enjoyment of looking for new falls with her husband; has kept her on a continual journey throughout Ohio, Indiana, and New York. Using her professional photographers keen eyesight and with the help of God's good grace, for rain, she used her passion for waterfalls and put together books for all to enjoy. When not traveling around the states looking for waterfalls or flowers, she resides near Cincinnati, Ohio with her husband, three cats, and Cockatoo Jake. Another hiking book will be coming out soon on Cleveland Ohio's Waterfalls!

Tom

Tina

9781257805198